The Black Athlete Revolt

The Black Athlete Revolt

The Sport Justice Movement in the Age of #BlackLivesMatter

Shaun M. Anderson

ROWMAN & LITTLEFIELD
Lanham • Boulder • New York • London

Published by Rowman & Littlefield
An imprint of The Rowman & Littlefield Publishing Group, Inc.
4501 Forbes Boulevard, Suite 200, Lanham, Maryland 20706
www.rowman.com

86-90 Paul Street, London EC2A 4NE, United Kingdom

British Library Cataloguing in Publication Information Available

Library of Congress Cataloging-in-Publication Data

Names: Anderson, Shaun M., 1983– author.
Title: The Black athlete revolt : the sport justice movement in the age of #BlackLivesMatter / Shaun M. Anderson.
Description: Lanham, MD : Rowman & Littlefield, [2022] | Includes bibliographical references and index. | Summary: "The Black Athlete Revolt is the first book to take a historical and contemporary look at how Black athletes have used their influence to move beyond protests and create substantial change for Black Americans. Spanning from the civil rights movement to today, this book reveals the ever-evolving and important role of Black athlete activism"—Provided by publisher.
Identifiers: LCCN 2022023346 (print) | LCCN 2022023347 (ebook) | ISBN 9781538153246 (cloth) | ISBN 9781538153253 (epub)
Subjects: LCSH: African American athletes—Political activity. | Black lives matter movement. | Sports—Social aspects—United States. | Social justice—United States. | United States—Race relations.
Classification: LCC GV706.32 .A54 2022 (print) | LCC GV706.32 (ebook) | DDC 796.089/96073—dc23/eng/20220630
LC record available at https://lccn.loc.gov/2022023346
LC ebook record available at https://lccn.loc.gov/2022023347

Contents

Foreword

I was born in New York City in 1952. I grew up in Section 8 housing with my parents and siblings until my parents were able to get better jobs. From there, we were able to move from Brooklyn to Queens. It was during this time that drugs, particularly heroin, ran rampant in my community. It caused a lot of turmoil in my family. Therefore, sports became my place for an escape. When I became a teenager, coaches in the community saw that I was 6'5" while the other kids were still under 6'0" tall. So they asked me if I would be interested in playing basketball. At first, it was a little difficult to learn the game, but by the time I reached my senior year of high school, I was an All-American.

By the end of the civil rights movement, the United States was focused on race and racial reconciliation and affirmative action. But I believe our society became complacent. The 1970s were the primary act of my professional career. After my NBA career ended in the late '80s, I went to law school. I pursued my law degree and went to fight apartheid in South Africa. I fought crime and drugs. I became a prosecutor because of this. In the state of Massachusetts, you were allowed to conduct preliminary hearings in your third year. I thought I was going to be a quality defense attorney fighting for justice. My third-year paper was on the *Batson v. Kentucky* case regarding loading juries with white jurors in cases where there were Black people on trial. Thurgood Marshall wrote the opinion and said it was discriminatory, and he filed a motion asking why it was legal to push Black people off of the jury in favor of whites. The only person to agree with me was Elizabeth Holtzman. I was then hired by her district attorney office. I worked with them for years on prosecuting police misconduct. That was thirty years ago and things have not changed. That colored my focus on justice work today.

I was also the CEO of iHoops, which was a joint venture between the NCAA and the NBA working to reform youth basketball. As we see it now, sport has morphed into a tightly woven piece of the American fabric—so tight that it is hard to distinguish the commercialism from the purity of sport. Where there is money to be made, you will have social and political influences. If you consider the Venn diagram, it would not be hard to see how those intersections work together. Social media and the zeal for most people to latch on to influencers are a part of the game as well. Think of the "Like Mike" movement during Michael Jordan's playing days. Owners of teams are billionaires, and because of their networks, you can utilize sport to have an influence on politics.

Given this, I teach athletics and social justice in the sport management program at Columbia University. I teach history and emphasize moments such as how organizations used *Plessy v. Ferguson* to eliminate Black athletes who were jockeys, cyclists, baseball players, and others from their particular sports. Back then, Black men scared white men. Jack Johnson comes to mind. You see, boxing was the epitome of masculinity. Boxing was considered a white man's sport. But Jack Johnson was relentless in claiming the championship. Paul Robeson, Jessie Owens, and Joe Louis were all athletes who fought for justice during the early parts of the twentieth century. I teach sport classes that show true history, and I try to teach individuals to have a positive impact. I don't pick up picket signs, but what I teach, what I espouse helps with individual thinking. I believe that small changes over time make a big difference.

Now I serve as cochair of the Knights Commission on Intercollegiate Athletics with former U.S. education secretary Arne Duncan and chancellor emeritus with the State University of New York, Nancy Zimpher. I chair a racial equity task force to research resources for issues that affect Black athletes, with the hope that this helps other marginalized athletes since many of the Black athletes are the ones who are the most commercialized! In this moment, in racial reckoning and reconciliation, there have been a lot of promises, but we want to move to policy change. We want to provide potential solutions that will bring about reform. We don't have enough policy reform. We want to put forth recommendations that will impress upon individual decision makers out there, whether it is the NCAA, college presidents, or athletic directors, to be better to society. It is very much a copycat industry, so if one changes, they all will. The challenge is to get people's attention. There has been a lack of equity, low graduation rates, exploitation, and bad experiences at predominantly white institutions (PWIs). Historically Black colleges and universities (HBCUs) bear the brunt of sanctions participating in postseason basketball due to low academic progress rates. Many of the students come from working-class families and have low resources. It becomes a problem. There are several disparities between PWIs and HBCUs when it comes to resources. But this work needs to be translated into professional sports as well.

It is time to rethink the way we use sport as an avenue to change society. The Black Lives Matter movement has risen and is taking a different direction from traditional organizations such as the NAACP and the civil rights movement. The symbolism is strong there. Black lives have to matter, and for far too long it seems they didn't. The symbolism of the movement illuminates the necessity of taking the issues of Black people seriously. Equity and equality, which are two different things, are very important. It pervades action, the symbolism not necessarily just the organization. The movement is just as important as the establishment of the institution. It is the fuel that keeps us going, that keeps me going. The movement and the message are both important. It is a slogan, but it is representative and impactful. I believe the slogan has more value than the organization, but there is no reason BLM the organization should not continue. People label it Marxist or socialist. If you look at history, the NAACP was labeled that, and MLK was labeled a communist. That is what the right wing and reactionaries try to do to disarm this type of movement as they try to label it as being antagonistic to democracy. We will get to that promised land.

There are several athletes who are doing powerful things since Black Lives Matter began. With this book, I hope it continues the conversation. We are a resilient people. We built this country. We are not deserting it. If it is not me, it will be my sons. That is the hope. We have to continue the dialogue. We cannot let it die like the civil rights movement died. If we do, we will pass another crime bill that has unintentional consequences against Black people. We must work to move forward. There is hope that things might change. Progress hasn't happened fast, but we have to keep pushing. We can't let up just because people have done a few things that have quieted the situation. Promises have to turn into policy. That is the definition of the movement. What is the structure? What are the goals? We want equity, we want change, but what are our goals? It cannot be broad and nebulous; you have to be focused and specific. If you are broad, it is like dancing in the dark. This book has illuminated the past, the present, and our needs for the future. I will continue the fight for justice, and I hope others will as well.

Len Elmore
NBA veteran, sportscaster, lawyer

Introduction

The early 1990s were a time when television networks were pushing for wholesome family values and public service announcements taught kids the negative consequences of using drugs. The reason for this was that America was dealing with a crack cocaine epidemic that created a surge in crime throughout inner-city America. It was a country divided as white people were blaming Black people for hurting their own communities, and Black people were blaming the federal government for introducing the drugs into their neighborhoods. To quell the turmoil, people turned to sport to escape their reality. This is not to say that the drug epidemic was the sole reason. By this time the professional sports world in the United States had reached global recognition. Tennis shoes named after athletes were just as popular as the players themselves. What was also at the height of its popularity was the relative silence of professional athletes when it came to social matters. One player's choice to speak up cost him everything.

Chris Jackson was born on March 9, 1969, in Gulfport, Mississippi, and was raised in a single-parent home. For much of his early life, Jackson struggled with health issues that went misdiagnosed until he reached high school. As a result of this, he was held back in the fourth grade and was eventually placed in special education classes. Despite his struggles, he would come under the tutelage of a local junior high school basketball coach who had noticed his skills during a pickup game. This coach would convince his mother to let him play organized basketball. By the time Jackson reached high school, he would be diagnosed with Tourette syndrome while simultaneously becoming a nationally known basketball phenom.

By his senior year, he was named a McDonald's All-American, which is one of the most prestigious honors high school basketball players can receive prior to playing college or professional basketball. He went on to accept a full scholarship to attend Louisiana State University (LSU). He earned freshman of the year, Southeastern Conference (SEC) player of the year, and first-team All-American by averaging over thirty points per game. During his sophomore year, he averaged nearly twenty-eight points per game while earning SEC player of the year and first-team All-American for the second straight year. After two stellar years at LSU, Jackson would declare for the NBA draft where he would eventually become the third overall pick in the NBA draft.

By 1993, Jackson had converted to Islam. Consequently, he would change his name to Mahmoud Abdul-Rauf. Through this change, Abdul-Rauf wanted to focus on ways to improve the plight of Black communities. It would be his religious beliefs that would change his career forever.

On March 10, 1996, the Denver Nuggets played a regular-season game against the New Jersey Nets. The teams were going through their routine pregame warm-ups prior to the start of the game. During the playing of the national anthem, all players stood, but Abdul-Rauf decided to sit. The reason for this was that he felt the American flag was "a symbol of tyranny, of oppression." Particularly, he explained that American customs were not parallel with his Islamic faith. In answering reports about his stance against oppression, he said,

> This country has a long history of that. I don't think you can argue the facts. You can't be for God and for oppression. It's clear in the Koran, Islam is the only way. I don't criticize those who stand, so don't criticize me for sitting. I won't waver from my decision.[1]

Two days later, NBA commissioner David Stern suspended Abdul-Rauf indefinitely. He would also sit out a game before he and the league settled on an agreement that he would stand for the anthem but he could bow his head to pray.

At the end of that season, the Nuggets would trade Abdul-Rauf, and within two years he was out of the NBA. Speculation would ensue that Abdul-Rauf was blackballed from the NBA because of his decision to protest the national anthem when any type of political protest of that magnitude was virtually obsolete. Furthermore, detractors of Abdul-Rauf would send him death threats, and racial slurs were hurled toward local mosques. The main aftermath of this incident was that no other athlete would challenge a professional sports franchise, let alone a sports league, for years to come. Still, Abdul-Rauf's NBA career was cut short after seven years. He would go on to play a few years for international basketball franchises before retiring and disappearing from the spotlight.

As we understand today's society, sports franchises and sport organizations can no longer stand silent as racism, inequality, and other social injustices continue to be detrimental to marginalized individuals. Whereas athletes in the 1990s remained cautious to attach their names to social causes, modern-day athletes have found solace in their reputations and their financial prowess to stand up for causes they believe in. It has been an interesting pathway to the revitalization of athlete activism, but there is still work to be done. This book examines how the Black Lives Matter movement served as a catalyst to revitalize athlete activism. In its near ten-year existence, the movement has been both lauded and criticized for what it stands for. But it has been one of the most substantial platforms in which athlete activists have found their voice.

In chapter 1, the history of the marriage between sports and politics is explored. Further, this chapter looks at how the American government failed on its promises of an equal America after the signing of the Emancipation Proclamation. It also discusses how political leaders from the early twentieth century to the civil rights movement galvanized athletes to stand up for social change during times in which their very lives were at stake. Lastly, the chapter discusses the dormancy of athlete activism after the civil rights movement.

Chapter 2 examines the Black Lives Matter movement, its purpose, and how it led to the revitalization of athlete activism. Chapter 3 focuses on how Colin Kaepernick and other high-profile athletes protested the national anthem, police brutality, and other instances of social injustice globally. Chapter 4 discusses how the revitalization of athlete activism provided an avenue to discuss policy reform. Chapter 5 introduces the sport justice movement as a new platform for social justice while providing insights from athletes and allies who discuss the future of athlete activism.

Chapter One

Sport and Politics: An Unholy Matrimony

"Does anyone object to this union?" These are often the words uttered by a priest as she or he gives final instruction for a couple to engage in holy matrimony. It is the last step for anyone to disagree with the joining of a couple before they spend the rest of their lives together in wedded bliss. Next comes the honeymoon, then comes reality. From then on, couples often live through endless opinions from friends and family, illness, disrespectful children, and other issues that may dominate a marriage. Like a marriage, the relationship between sport and politics has gone through its fair share of ebbs and flows.

You see, there has been this constant outcry bemoaning the relationship between sport and politics for decades. Mostly, those who are against the union say that sport should only be an avenue for entertaining the masses. They further suggest that the athletes who engage in these acts of political demonstration are ignorant about societal ills and are not intelligent enough to speak on them. Consequently, they are relegated to being perceived as mindless imbeciles who should simply destroy their bodies for the sake of entertainment.

To speak frankly, the issue of sport and politics has been mostly a white person versus Black athlete issue. For decades, Black athletes have expressed their discontent with issues such as police brutality, inequality, racism, lynching, and systematic oppression, only to be met with opposition. It has cost many of these athletes their livelihoods and, sadly, their lives. While this is a tumultuous union, it was an inevitable one. But what led us to this disastrous union? Why are Black athletes still having to defend their right to protest? The answer can be found in the mid-nineteenth century after America fought its internal battle.

THE AUDACITY OF THE BLACK EXODUS

The American Civil War (1861–1865) represented a culmination of the fight to end slavery in the United States. During the war, President Abraham Lincoln wrote the Emancipation Proclamation (1863), which further acknowledged the abolishment of slavery. Although it was extremely flawed, the proclamation allowed for African Americans to join the Union military to combat the Confederacy throughout the rest of the war. While the Union claimed victory at the end of the war, African Americans still faced a harsh road ahead.

A few months before the Civil War ended, the U.S. Congress passed the Thirteenth Amendment, which officially abolished slavery. As America worked to restore the nation from the turmoil of the war, Black people continued the fight for equality. Dubbed the Reconstruction era (1865–1977), Black people faced increased segregation, violence, and political uprisings, mostly from white men who were members of the Confederate military. While the passing of the Fourteenth and Fifteenth Amendments granted equal protection under the law and granted people of all colors the right to vote, respectively, segregationist and white supremacist leanings remained a larger part of the daily struggle for Black people.

While America was going through Reconstruction after the Civil War, newly freed slaves were waiting for the promises of the Emancipation Proclamation to be fulfilled. But after a few years of continued discrimination, many of these freed slaves turned to sports for economic empowerment. On May 17, 1875, Col. Meriwether Lewis Clark Jr., who was the grandson of William Clark of the Lewis and Clark expedition, developed a horse-racing competition in Louisville, Kentucky, after learning of its popularity in France. Titled the Kentucky Derby, Clark saw this as an opportunity to profit from the burgeoning growth of sports in the United States. Interestingly, the jockeys were African American. These men raced horses because they grew up on plantations to parents who tended the horse stables. Given this familiarity with horses and their temperament, horse racing quickly grew in popularity in the African American community. One of the more popular jockeys was Isaac Murphy. Murphy was born into slavery on January 6, 1861. His father died not too long after the Civil War, which prompted Isaac and his mother to move in with Eli Jordan, a family friend. Jordan was a prominent horse trainer for the Williams and Owings horse stables. It was here that Murphy began to see a path to success.

At the age of fourteen, Murphy began learning the basics of horse riding while under Jordan's tutelage. Ten years later, Murphy would be one of several Black jockeys who would compete in the Kentucky Derby. He would go on to win his first competition in 1884, and by 1891 he had won three Kentucky Derby championships. After his successes, Murphy would become one of the world's most famous athletes. However, societal grumblings would ensue as Jim Crow laws and continued violence against Black people led to many changes in the sport. In the prime of his career, Murphy succumbed to heart failure in 1896 at the age of thirty-five. His death, along with the Supreme Court making segregation into law that same year via the *Plessy v. Ferguson* case, spelled doom for Black jockeys.

The *Plessy v. Ferguson* court case (1896) decided that segregation should remain constitutional regarding the use of public facilities, provided that Black people were able to use facilities of equal quality. This landmark case reinforced local and state laws created after the Civil War that controlled where formerly enslaved people could work, how much they earned, how they voted, where they lived, and how they were educated. Called the Jim Crow era (circa 1865–1968), America became embattled with a war between white nationalists who preferred domination over others and Black people who continued the fight toward equality.

Many Black jockeys were earning what would be considered millions in today's dollars. While Murphy was arguably the most dominant jockey in his day, several other prominent Black jockeys excelled at the sport. But by the early 1900s, several found themselves struggling to cope with America's segregation policies. Depressed and hopeless, many of these athletes had tragic endings. James "Soup" Perkins, who won the Kentucky Derby when he was fifteen years old, died of excessive alcohol consumption at the age of thirty-one in 1911. Albert Isom, who was a prominent racer, publicly shot himself in the head after he could no longer find work. Thomas Britton, who won the Tennessee Derby, committed suicide by swallowing acid when he was kept away from racing.

Now these athletes are a distant memory. They had the capabilities necessary to help their families, friends, and community, and it was all taken away from them. The elite Black athlete became obsolete. This could arguably be considered the first instance in which sport and politics collided, albeit unintentionally. While athletes at the time were not involved in politics, the legal system intervened in their livelihoods, which would wreak havoc for years to come. While this era saw increased violence against Black people who fought for their rights, some Black leaders emerged who claimed that the only way to true freedom and equality was to leave America altogether.

Born in 1887 to a somewhat well-to-do Jamaican family, Marcus Garvey became one of the pioneers of Black liberation and one of the first to declare a mass exodus from America. In learning the concepts of unionizing and the power of the media in his youth, Garvey established the Universal Negro

Improvement Association (UNIA) in 1914 as a platform to end European control of Africa and galvanize Black people across the diaspora under one politically unified ideal within the continent.[1] After various travels throughout the Caribbean and other European colonies where people of African descent were living, he decided to further establish his organization by moving to Harlem, New York. As head of what was now called the Universal Negro Improvement Association and African Communities League (UNIA-ACL), Garvey declared that the only way the American Negro could find freedom and equality was to join members of the global diaspora in their move to Africa under one political regime.

Within a decade, Garvey's UNIA-ACL became a threat to imperialistic authorities throughout Africa. Further, his newspaper, *The Negro World*, showcased the political and artistic talents of individuals from the African diaspora. As a result, the newspaper became a catalyst for the Harlem Renaissance and galvanized members of the diaspora to recognize their power to resist European colonization as one united Africa. Officially termed as "Garveyism," the threat of a movement back to Africa spelled doom for European leaders who sought sustainable control over various African countries.[2]

At the height of the movement, the thought of African nationalism materialized globally while several African leaders began to see the continued struggle of Africans in the Western Hemisphere. It was reported that the king of Swaziland told Garvey's wife, Amy Jacques Garvey, that he knew of only two prominent Black figures in the West: Marcus Garvey and Jack Johnson.[3]

Johnson, a boxer who became the first African American world heavyweight champion from 1908 to 1915, was neither a statesman nor a politician. However, he was known for his brash, intimidating persona with a blatant disregard for white supremacy. Standing at 6'2", Johnson further intimidated white people by living a boisterously lavish lifestyle that included marrying white women and calling out white boxers who were afraid to challenge him. At the height of his career, Johnson had defeated several white opponents. His most prominent victory was in 1910 against former boxing champion James J. Jeffries, who was retired but was out to prove that the white man was better than the Negro. Dubbed the "Fight of the Century," the fight represented America's "great white hope" of defeating Johnson.[4] However, Johnson defeated Jeffries, which further established Johnson's boxing prowess, but it also exacerbated racial tensions.

No doubt due to Johnson's tendency to humiliate white people at any chance, the result of the fight caused riots between Black people, who felt a collective sense of victory, and white people, who felt embarrassed by Jefferies's defeat. Overall, approximately twenty-five states across the United States were involved in the riots, with over one hundred people being either killed or injured. It was during this time that sport and politics began to flirt with each other. While Garvey and Johnson never met, each of their respective ways in handling white supremacy represented a revolutionist way of Black liberation. While seemingly unintentional, Garvey's thoughts on Black liberation and Johnson's brute force developed a matrimony that would situate Black athletes as both superior and as political beacons of hope that spoke to athletes recognizing their power to revolt against white supremacy.

Garvey's attack on European colonization and Johnson's lack of fear toward white America were the catalysts for members of the African diaspora to recognize their power to seek liberation. Although Garvey's attempt to repatriate members of the diaspora back to Africa failed, it had a lasting impact on political and religious movements worldwide. Also, Johnson's victory against Jeffries would make him a target of increased racial tension for the rest of his life. But he helped set the stage for athletes to use their voices as platforms to address social inequality despite his aversion to speaking on such issues.

THE TALLEST TREE IN THE FOREST

Although Garvey's back-to-Africa movement was arguably one of the boldest actions toward racial progress, he was not the only Black leader during this time. For example, Ida B. Wells, a pioneering journalist and educator, wrote tirelessly about race and politics throughout the southern United States. Booker T. Washington, a former slave and educator, founded Tuskegee University as an institution for Black people to remain separate while seeking socioeconomic equality from their white counterparts. Mary McLeod Bethune, an educator, philanthropist, and civil rights leader, cofounded the United Negro College Fund and developed an all-girls school that would eventually become Bethune-Cookman University. W. E. B. DuBois, the first Black Harvard PhD graduate and sociologist, cofounded the National Association for the Advancement of Colored People (NAACP). While all were about racial progress, they often held conflicting views as to how to get there. Still, they used their various platforms to challenge discriminatory policies that thwarted equality. However, there was one leader who combined his athletic talents and legal acumen to expand upon Garvey's globalized efforts of liberation.

Paul LeRoy Robeson was born in 1898 in Princeton, New Jersey, to a mother who was a former slave and a father who was an ex-Union officer.[5] As a youth, Robeson excelled in several areas, including the arts, athletics, and academics. Robeson was so gifted that he attended Rutgers College in New Brunswick, New Jersey (now Rutgers University), on an academic scholarship while becoming the school's first Black football player. By the time he graduated in 1919, he was named his class's valedictorian while also earning a place on the College Football All-America Team two times. After this, Robeson went on to play professional football and performed in a traveling theater company that often traveled globally to perform. These were his areas of interest, but they also served as a means to fund his true passion: the pursuance of a law degree. His girlfriend at the time, Eslanda "Essie" Goode, convinced him to continue working in the theater because she recognized his immense talent. By 1921 he and Goode married, and in 1923 he graduated from Columbia Law School and immediately began practicing law. Much to his chagrin, Robeson found the racism levied against him for practicing law intolerable, and he soon quit to pursue a career in theater full time.

By the 1930s, Garvey's philosophy on Black liberation was fading, and Robeson began to grow in prominence. Like Garvey, Robeson spent much of his time traveling globally. However, it was not initially spent on engaging in activism. He toured Britain as a concert artist, performing in several well-known acts such as *Othello* and "Ol' Man River."[6] He became famous throughout Europe as both an artist and a burgeoning activist. One of his first acts of activism was donating a part of his salary to the Welsh miners' relief fund that provided care to the families of over two hundred miners who had died in an underground fire accident. In addition to this, he helped establish negotiations for labor rights with the Welsh union. It was at this point that Robeson began to find his political footing.

As his fame grew throughout Europe, Robeson began to recognize that his platform as an artist could draw attention to issues of the day. For example, one of his first attempts to eradicate inequality was by challenging British colonialism globally. He would soon be invited to many European countries to perform and further establish his activism. It was in the Soviet Union during one of his performances that he developed a liking for their political views, particularly the constitution, which declared the eradication of inequity among all of its citizens. Consequently, he embraced the Marxist method of political thought, which is considered the uprising of the lower class over the upper class to control production as a way to eradicate social classes.[7] Specifically, Robeson believed that Russia was a haven for African Americans who sought refuge from racial oppression in the United States. He stated that in Russia he was treated like a human being, with dignity and respect. It would be this ideology that would guide his activism for the rest of his life.

By the late 1930s, Robeson had fully embraced his role as an artist-activist. He proclaimed that "the artist must take sides. He must elect to fight for freedom or slavery. I have made my choice. I had no alternative."[8] With this thought process, he would visit several countries (e.g., China, Scotland, Spain, South Africa) on various issues such as human rights, labor rights, and colonialism. However, his true passion was the fight for the freedom of members of the African diaspora. He cofounded, along with African American communist Max Yergan, the Council of African Affairs (CAA). Along with prominent leaders such as W. E. B. DuBois, the CAA was one of the largest organizations that fought against colonialism and apartheid for the diaspora.

Whereas Garvey sought the complete emancipation and repatriation of Black people back to Africa, Robeson sought liberation through integration and equality. As such, he met with leaders at the United Nations and with U.S. presidents who called these leaders to action relating to racism and freedom. Also dissimilar to Garvey's ideology was the fact that Robeson denounced the notion of Black people repatriating from the United States and viewed race only as a social construct. When asked why he did not stay in Russia, he replied, "Because my father was a slave, and my people died to build this country, and I am going to stay here and have a part of it just like you. And no fascist-minded people will drive me from it. Is that clear?"[9]

By the late 1940s, Robeson was at the height of his fame and influence. He was at the forefront of equality and freedom among the African diaspora, prominent Black leaders (e.g., DuBois, McLeod Bethune) partnered with him, and his performances were world renowned. Despite this, his sociopolitical leanings came under scrutiny. The United States recognized Russia as a deserter during World War I and vehemently opposed the country's communist politics. As mentioned, Robeson believed that the Russian model of politics would serve Black people well in their quest for racial freedom. Consequently, he became someone that the U.S. government needed to keep under control. As a result, President Harry S. Truman approved the order to revoke Robeson's passport, eliminating his influence in political affairs and performances globally in 1950.

For nearly a decade, Robeson's blacklisting by the U.S. government severely limited the way he earned a living. Despite this, he would continue to fight for the global freedom of Black people. By 1958, the *Kent v. Dulles* court case allowed for his passport to be restored, as it protected First Amendment rights regarding free speech.[10] He soon moved back to Europe to begin performing again while also fighting for global equality. However, the effects of his banishment took a toll on his health. He would often have severe bouts of paranoia and depression due to his thoughts of being killed by the U.S. government. He was even warned not to return to the United States because of his continued global fight for equality.

Within five years of his passport being reinstated, Robeson's health deteriorated even more. By 1963 he finally returned to the United States. For most of his life, Robeson fought for the freedoms of the African diaspora. He represented the quintessential Renaissance man: an athlete, scholar, lawyer, artist, and activist. Some scholars described him as "the blueprint of human existence."[11] Because of his influence, he had helped galvanize a new social movement within the United States that saw the rise of many prominent Black leaders toward the fight for racial freedom and equality.

A LEAGUE OF THEIR OWN

While members of the African diaspora were divided on Garvey's push for a unified return to Africa and Robeson's global push for equality, America saw the rise of its national pastime. Although it originated in the nineteenth century, baseball became popular on a national level in the early twentieth century. From 1900 to 1920, several white and Black leaders established baseball organizations that featured predominantly Black players. One of the more established organizations was the National Association of Colored Baseball Clubs of the United States and Cuba. It was established in 1907 to provide a sense of order and balance to burgeoning Black baseball organizations. The league quickly folded, leaving Black baseball an unorganized entity. It wasn't until a Texas native with a strong right arm arrived that the popularity of Black baseball was firmly cemented.

Andrew "Rube" Foster was born in 1879 to sharecropper parents. Early on, he developed a penchant for the game of baseball. By the early 1900s, he was a prominent pitcher for several Black baseball teams, in particular the Chicago American Giants. During Foster's playing career, the Giants became one of the winningest franchises in Black baseball history. By 1911, Foster became owner, player, and manager of the Giants, and the team continued to dominate. Noticing a need for an established league that focused on the growth of Black baseball and Black economic empowerment, Foster established the Negro National League in 1920.

It was at this time, in 1920, that the white Major League Baseball (MLB) owners elected Kenesaw Mountain Landis to be the organization's first commissioner. Landis, who was elected by President Theodore Roosevelt as a U.S. district court judge for the Northern District of Illinois in 1905, was known as a no-nonsense presence whose mission was to end corruption in big business. Landis brought that same law and order to the game of baseball, but he was also accused of keeping the game segregated. Landis and team owners did not establish a formalized policy that kept Black players from playing in MLB, but there was a common understanding or "gentleman's agreement" of such a ruling. So Black people established a league of their own, the Negro National League.

By the mid-1920s, the Negro National League became a nationally known pastime for Black Americans, even beginning to rival the popularity of Major League Baseball. The league would also establish the Colored World Series, which became one of the more popular events in American history. Unfortunately, Foster's health deteriorated when he accidentally inhaled fumes from a leaky gas pipe while touring for one of his team's games. This accident caused him to act erratically, so much so that he was committed to an insane asylum in Illinois where he would die in 1930.

As a result of Foster's death and the rise of the Great Depression, the Negro National League folded in 1930. However, his leadership established Black baseball as a nationally known phenomenon that provided Black athletes an avenue for growth and popularity separate from Major League Baseball. By the mid-1930s, the Negro Leagues were reestablished and lasted nearly thirty years. It established an even stronger presence than its predecessor and posed a major threat to overtake the popularity of its white counterpart, a threat that Major League Baseball had to remove.

SPORT AS A PRECURSOR

As Robeson's influence was on the decline due to being blacklisted, several major events in the sports world to combat racial inequity emerged. Jackie Robinson would start a chain reaction that led to one of the most powerful movements in American history. Robinson was born on January 13, 1919, in a small city in Georgia. Shortly after he was born, his family moved to Pasadena, California, to seek out better opportunities. While a teenager, several people noticed his athletic gifts. As a result, he was encouraged to pursue organized sports. He would excel at several sports, including basketball, football, baseball, track, and tennis. He would do so well that by the end of his high school career he had won multiple tennis and baseball championships.

After high school, Robinson would attend Pasadena Junior College (PJC) where he would continue to excel in multiple sports. He graduated from PJC in 1939 and went on to enroll in one of the few integrated colleges in the country: the University of California at Los Angeles (UCLA). There, he would become the only varsity athlete to earn letters in four different sports: football, track, baseball, and basketball. Despite his athletic trajectory, Robinson decided to leave UCLA before graduating.

After stints of playing semiprofessional football and working as a youth sports athletic director, he would enroll in the U.S. Army in 1942. Robinson's time in the military would only last two years. He was arrested when he refused to move to the back of a military bus at the request of the driver. The incident led to Robinson being court-martialed. He was eventually acquitted of all charges but was honorably discharged. He went on to serve a stint as an athletics director and basketball coach for Samuel Huston College. It was an invitation from a Negro League baseball team that would change the trajectory of Robinson's life along with changing the nation.

In 1945, Robinson was sent a letter by the Kansas City Monarchs of the Negro Leagues formally inviting him to play for the team. Although baseball was not his best sport at UCLA, he would play well with the Monarchs despite not being the best Negro League player. However, the Negro Leagues were less organized than his time at UCLA. This, along with the grueling travel schedule, would increase his frustrations with the league. Consequently, he sought out the unprecedented: a Major League Baseball contract.

The Boston Red Sox would be one of the first teams in Major League Baseball to try out Black players.[12] Robinson tried out with them but quickly learned that the tryout was a publicity stunt to help quell protests against segregation. Although disappointed, Robinson would get another chance. The Brooklyn Dodgers' general manager and president Branch Rickey began to explore a more serious route to integration within baseball. Recognizing the popularity and showmanship of the Negro Leagues, he saw an opportunity to take advantage.

There were several issues that Rickey had to account for. First, how could a league that held a gentlemen's agreement to keep Black players out of the game finally evolve? Second, how would a Black player handle the perceived scrutiny he would face from teammates, opponents, and fans? Finally, how would allowing a Black player into the game affect revenue? Rickey knew that he could not select any random player. Rather, the player chosen would have to be able to adjust to the Major Leagues both mentally and physically.

In understanding this, Rickey would reach out to Robinson to discuss the possibility of him playing the sport. In the conversation, Rickey tested Robinson by hurling racial epithets at him to see how he would react. Reluctantly, Robinson signed with the Dodgers' minor league affiliate, the Montreal Royals. Throughout the 1946 season, Robinson would face intense scrutiny from his Royals coaches and teammates. However, he would persevere in preparation for his Major League debut.

On April 15, 1947, Robinson would make history as the first African American baseball player in the Major Leagues since MLB became officially organized in 1904. Throughout his rookie season, Robinson's tenure was met with bouts of extreme racism. But his appearance in the Major Leagues would begin to draw Black crowds away from the Negro Leagues. Consequently, the Negro Leagues, vendors associated with the league, and Black newspaper outlets that covered the league began to suffer. Although the integration of Major League Baseball ultimately led to the demise of the Negro Leagues, Robinson's sacrifice would not be in vain.

Robinson's integration of Major League Baseball was a major first step for Black athletes. But his influence went beyond the diamond. In 1949, Robinson was asked to testify in Washington, DC, before the House Un-American Activities Committee against Robeson. Robeson's frequent global lectures on racism continued to permeate throughout the United States. As Robinson was considered a model "American Negro," the government felt that in testifying against Robeson, Robinson would quell any revolt that Black people might conceive under the guise of communist leanings. In his testimony, Robinson said,

> White people must realize that the more a Negro hates Communism because it opposes democracy, the more he is going to hate any other influence that kills off democracy in this country and that goes for racial discrimination in the Army, and segregation on trains and buses, and job discrimination of religious beliefs or color or place of birth. And one other thing the American public ought to understand, if we are to make progress in this matter: The fact that it is a Communist who denounces injustice in the courts, police brutality, and lynching when it happens doesn't change the truth of his charges. Just because communists kick up a big fuss over racial discrimination when it suits their purposes, a lot of people try to pretend that the whole issue is a creation of Communist imagination. But they are not fooling anyone with this kind of pretense, and talk about Communists stirring up Negroes to protest only makes present misunderstanding worse than ever. Negroes were stirred up long before there was a Communist Party, and they'll stay stirred up long after the party has disappeared—unless Jim Crow has disappeared by then as well.[13]

This statement, while meant to be the governments' plot to have high-profile Black athletes denounce Robeson, showed that Black people wanted to stay united to fight inequality despite differing ideologies. Within a decade of Jackie Robinson's groundbreaking entrance into Major League Baseball, several prominent Black athletes began breaking the proverbial glass ceiling. One in particular was tennis star Althea Gibson.[14] Born on August 15, 1927, in South Carolina, Gibson was the daughter of sharecroppers. During the Great Depression, her parents moved to Harlem, New York, to seek out better opportunities for them and their children.

At an early age, Gibson was recognized for her athletic gifts, so her parents got her involved in organized sports. Her parents would get her involved in the Police Athletic League in her neighborhood that would block out certain times of the day so that neighborhood kids could play. Through this, Gibson would develop an interest in paddle tennis. She became so proficient that by the age of twelve she had won the New York City women's paddle tennis championship. She would go on to face several hardships throughout her teenage years, including dropping out of school. But she continued to find solace in tennis. She continued to hone her gifts. By the age of twenty, she had won multiple American Tennis Association (ATA) championship matches.[15] The ATA, which is the oldest African American sports organization in the United States, showcased her raw talent. But one person saw that she should achieve more.

Dr. R. Walter Johnson, who was a physician and advocate of African Americans playing tennis, decided to take Gibson under his mentorship. He would connect Gibson to Hubert Eaton, who was another supporter of African American tennis. Eaton would convince Gibson to reenroll in school so that she could have a better route to play professional tennis. In 1949, after high school, she would enroll at Florida A&M University on an athletic scholarship, where she would continue to hone her skills.

Shortly thereafter, Gibson began receiving national attention for her tennis skills. However, racial segregation and other discriminatory practices banned Black people from participating in national tournaments. During this time, the largest tennis tournament in the United States was the U.S. National Championships (Nationals).[16] Now called the U.S. Open, it was an organization that allowed participants to gain entrance into the tournament by qualifying through smaller sanctioned tournaments that were often held in private, whites-only clubs.

After receiving a note admonishing the tournament's discriminatory practices, the Nationals opened their tournament to players of all ethnicities. As a result, Gibson became the first African American to receive an invitation to play in the tournament. Although Gibson would lose her first match to Nationals winner Louise Brough, the match placed her in the global conversation on race and sport. Gibson's impact on breaking the color barrier in women's tennis was so profound that Lester Rodney, who was a prominent writer for the *Daily Worker*, would draw comparisons to Jackie Robinson. He went on to say,

No negro player man or woman, has ever set foot on these courts. . . . In many ways, it is even a tougher personal Jim Crow–busting assignment than was Jackie Robinson's when he first stepped out of the Brooklyn Dodgers dugout.[17]

In 1956, Gibson would become a household name when she became the first African American to win a Grand Slam title. The next year, she won at Wimbledon and the Nationals. In 1958, she would repeat as a champion for both Wimbledon and the Nationals. Despite her fame and inspiring path to being a champion, racial discrimination, and regulations regarding the rights of amateur players earning money from playing tennis, Gibson would retire to pursue other interests. However, her story would go on to inspire other people of color to pursue tennis as an outlet for success. While she was not outspoken about her politics, her actions to pursue equality in tennis spoke volumes throughout the tennis world.

Still, Black people were seeking more than integration. Rather, they wanted the eradication of policies that denied them their basic inalienable rights. The burgeoning question at that time was, by what means do they obtain these rights? One leader would find solace in Robeson's philosophy.

THE CIVIL RIGHTS MOVEMENT

Bayard Rustin was born in 1912 in Pennsylvania to parents who were influential members of the African Methodist Episcopal Church (AME) and the NAACP. Due to his upbringing, he became highly aware of the Jim Crow laws that stifled Black progress within the United States. He would use this awareness to develop a unique political ideology. To hone his skills in political protest, Rustin became the mentee of A. Philip Randolph, a union leader and socialist who developed the first successful African American union. Additionally, he found another mentor in A. J. Muste, a minister and pacifist who taught him the principles of peace and nonviolence practiced by Mahatma Gandhi. Through these mentorships, Rustin became a master strategist who helped pave the way for the civil rights movement. One of his first tasks was to develop the youth movement strategy for the 1941 March on Washington, a march dedicated to ending labor segregation in preparation for World War II. The result of the planned march influenced then-president Franklin D. Roosevelt to issue an executive order denouncing labor segregation of African Americans. Consequently, Randolph called off the march, much to the chagrin of Rustin's radical preferences.

Shortly after this time, Rustin fully emerged as a pacifist antiwar critic, orator, and civil disobedience strategist who began to move away from socialist leanings. He would be hired by Muste in 1943 to serve as an organizing strategist for the Fellowship of Reconciliation (FOR), a Christian pacifist group. This, along with his Quaker upbringing, helped him become one of the leading antiwar and anti-violence leaders in the United States. His beliefs against war were so prominent that he ended up serving two years in Kentucky and Pennsylvania federal prisons for violating the Selective Service Act. Upon his release from prison in 1946, Rustin continued his work with FOR. Like Robeson, he expanded his activism by visiting countries such as India, Africa, and Europe, denouncing war and colonialism. While Rustin's reputation as a radical pacifist and strategist was growing, he was arrested in 1953 for public indecency when he was caught having sex with a man in a parked car. Although openly gay, it was considered illegal to engage in sex acts with someone of the same gender. As a result of public ridicule, he would spend the remainder of his life engaged in activism from behind the scenes. Rustin was quickly let go from FOR due to his public indecency arrest. However, he was able to reconcile with Randolph and was tasked with developing a strategy that would be the spark for the civil rights movement.

In 1955, Rustin was introduced to a young minister named Martin Luther King Jr. who was trying to lead a bus boycott in Mobile, Alabama. The purpose of the boycott was in response to the arrest of Rosa Parks, who refused to give up her seat to a white passenger. With King's lack of organizing skills, Rustin would provide him with the guidance and mentorship that led to a successful boycott between 1955 and 1956. The boycott would subsequently lead to the *Browder v. Gayle* (1956) court decision that declared racial segregation laws for buses unconstitutional.

Due to the success of the march, Rustin began to envision a grand movement throughout the southern United States that would galvanize many leaders to fight for policy reform. However, his homosexuality and former socialist leanings made him a liability to be at the forefront of the movement. Therefore he would continue to serve as a strategist and visionary while King and others emerged as spokespersons for the movement. To aid in convening several prominent southern Black leaders under one regime, Rustin helped King formulate the Southern Christian Leadership Conference (SCLC) one year after the boycotts ended.

By the 1960s the civil rights movement was at its height. Rustin, in his attempt to help Robeson enjoy the fruits of his labor regarding his work on Black liberation, invited him to join the movement. Robeson declined because he was asked to denounce his communist leanings. As the movement persisted, two polarizing figures became the face of the movement: Martin Luther King Jr. and Malcolm X. Rustin would continue to work with King as a strategist on the fight for equality and integration. However, Malcolm X aligned with the Nation of Islam, which focused on Black empowerment, liberation, and segregation by any means necessary. For most of the movement, King and Malcolm X opposed one another's methods for Black liberation. Despite this, their causes would be the catalyst for the largest Black athlete revolt in U.S. history.

FROM BALLERS TO ACTIVISTS

The civil rights movement was rife with Black leaders who were fed up with the prejudice and discrimination that continued to permeate the United States. Likewise, several Black athletes aimed at these critical issues. One championed the fight for justice both on and off the basketball court. William Felton Russell, commonly known as Bill, was born on February 12, 1934, in Monroe, Louisiana. Like many Black families that lived in the highly segregated South, Russell and his family moved to the San Francisco Bay Area. There, coaches noticed his height and compelled him to play basketball.

During high school, Russell played center for McClymonds High School in Oakland, California. While not the best player at the time, his height and build allowed him to earn a scholarship at the nearby University of San Francisco. It was there that Russell honed his skills, winning NCAA national championships in 1955 and 1956, respectively. By his senior year, he became a defensive specialist who was a consistent scorer, which garnered interest from several NBA teams.

The Boston Celtics would eventually draft him in the first round, and after a brief stint playing for the U.S. Olympic team in Melbourne, he joined the team. He adapted quickly to the NBA style and helped bring the Celtics their first championship during the 1956–1957 season. By 1960, the Russell-led Celtics had won multiple NBA championships, setting them up as a dynasty. Simultaneously, the civil rights movement was reaching its height, and Russell felt compelled to use his platform to create social change.

In 1961, Russell encouraged his Black teammates to boycott an exhibition game against the St. Louis Hawks when he and the others were refused service at a hotel coffee shop. Two years later, he stood with Martin Luther King Jr. during the March on Washington and had a front-row seat during his famous "I Have a Dream" speech. In 1966, Russell continued his illustrious basketball career by succeeding legendary Celtics coach Red Auerbach as head coach. This move made him the first Black head coach across all professional U.S. sports. After three years of serving as both player and coach, Russell retired a perennial all-star who had led the Celtics to eleven championships in thirteen years. He continued to serve as a representative for the NBA and civil rights well beyond his playing career.

During the prime of Russell's playing career, other athletes became defiant against America's continued reign of segregation and discrimination against Black people. One notable athlete followed in Russell's footsteps as both an NBA player and an activist. Kareem Abdul-Jabbar was born Ferdinand Lewis Alcindor Jr. on April 16, 1947, in Harlem, New York. At birth, he weighed nearly thirteen pounds and was almost two feet long. His unique size would continue throughout his early years. By the age of ten, he was nearly 6'0" tall. When he was in his early teens, he was 6'8" and was being sought out by coaches to play basketball. Over the next few years, he became a high school basketball star. He led the Power Memorial Academy High School to two New York City Catholic championships by the time he graduated from high school in 1965. It was once he got to college that he invoked his prowess for activism.

Abdul-Jabbar decided to attend UCLA to play college basketball but had to sit out during his first year, as freshmen were banned from playing varsity basketball until a rule change in 1972. He made his on-court debut during his sophomore season and immediately became a star. Under head coach John Wooden, he led the team to a 30–0 record, along with winning the national championship in 1967. Known for his dominating style of dunking the basketball, the NCAA instituted a new rule at the end of the 1966–1967 season that banned players from dunking. Many considered this rule a discriminatory practice that would hinder his growth as a player. Nonetheless, Abdul-Jabbar would continue his dominance throughout his college career.

In 1968, he utilized his stardom as an avenue to create social change on multiple levels. First, he relinquished his name of origin and adopted his current name when he converted from Catholicism to Islam. The reason behind Abdul-Jabbar's name change was due to his interest in Malcolm X's teachings on Black empowerment, pride, and self-help. One of his first acts under his new name was to boycott the 1968 Olympics, to which he had previously been invited to represent the United States in basketball. He explained that the reason behind the boycott was that he did not understand the point of winning a gold medal for a country that continued to keep Black people oppressed. He even delivered a lecture titled "The Myth of America as a Melting Pot" during a class early on in his time at UCLA.

Upon completion of his undergraduate major in 1969, he declared for the NBA draft. He would finish his college career with multiple national championships and be voted the first-ever Naismith College player of the year. He was selected first overall by the Milwaukee Bucks and spent his first six seasons with the team. In 1975, he was traded to the Los Angeles Lakers, where he would spend fourteen years, ultimately becoming one of the best players in NBA history. Throughout his playing career, he continued to fight for racial justice both on and off the court through his writing, books, and calling out those who continued to oppress marginalized individuals. Russell and Abdul-Jabbar both continue to speak on and fight against racial oppression well beyond their retirement years, so much so that former president Barack Obama awarded the Presidential Medal of Freedom to Russell in 2011 and Abdul-Jabbar in 2016 for their continued work on eradicating social injustice.

PAR FOR THE COURSE

During the civil rights era, golf was considered a whites-only sport. However, Charlie Sifford would change that.[18] Sifford was born on June 2, 1922, in Charlotte, North Carolina. As a youth, he served as a caddie to a white golfer at a North Carolina country club and quickly honed his skills. Later he began playing on the whites-only golf course, much to the chagrin of the club's patrons. At the age of seventeen, he left North Carolina and move to Philadelphia, Pennsylvania, due to an incident in which a white male was hurling racial slurs. While in Philadelphia, Sifford competed with other Black golfers and further honed his skills. With no other prospects, he enlisted in the U.S. Army and served in the segregated arm of the military during World War II. Upon his return, he had a chance encounter with Jackie Robinson that would help change the trajectory of golf.

Sifford, who idolized Jackie Robinson, confessed that he had a lifelong dream of breaking the color barrier in golf.[19] Robinson would advise Sifford regarding the perils of racism and the death threats he would receive if he attempted to do it. However, he challenged Sifford not to quit in the pursuit. In 1948, Sifford tried to seek entrance into whites-only tournaments but was ultimately denied. Therefore, he would compete in the Black golf tournaments. He excelled in the United Golf Association's National Negro Open where he became the tournament's winningest competitor. Still, he continued to pursue his goal of breaking the color barrier.

The Professional Golfers' Association (PGA) of America, which was established in 1916, is the nation's largest authority that serves the profession of golf. In 1934, the PGA established a "whites-only clause" within their bylaws that said people of color were banned from playing in any tournament hosted by the association. By 1952, Sifford and others had made progress when the PGA allowed them to play in the Phoenix Open, which is one in a series of nationwide tour stops professional golfers played in. Unfortunately, when Sifford and his golf mates began to play, they found excrement in one of their golf holes. Other golfers would also challenge the clause, and in 1955 the U.S. Supreme Court would hear their case. However, the court upheld the bylaws established.

By 1957, the PGA came under further scrutiny. Sifford was granted admission to play in the Long Beach Open, which was not an official PGA tournament member but was sanctioned by the association. He won the tournament in a play-off, which caused several people to question the legitimacy of the clause. California state attorney Stanley Mosk and Sifford convened to discuss the unfair treatment he received in trying to compete in major tournaments, and

Mosk challenged the PGA to change their bylaws or risk being banned from playing their tournament in the state of California.

In 1960, the PGA responded to the constant threats by adding Sifford as an approved player who could compete in their tournaments. The following year, the efforts by Sifford and Mosk would force the PGA to eradicate its clause from their official bylaws, which opened up major golf tournaments to all people of color. For the next decade, Sifford would go on to win multiple tournaments despite continued racial hostility beyond the elimination of the clause. His sacrifices would catalyze other integration efforts across the country.

I AIN'T GOT NO QUARREL
WITH THEM VIETCONG

As the movement grew, it became increasingly multifaceted. The focus was not only on equal rights for Black people. It began to shift to labor rights, rights for voting, and education, to name a few. The landmark *Brown v. Board of Education* case, which declared separate but equal educational institutions unconstitutional, spawned the end of the Jim Crow laws that had been established previously with the *Plessy v. Ferguson* case. The Civil Rights Act of 1964 further established that discrimination in areas such as employment, education, and voting was unconstitutional. Still, Black people were met with hostility as protests and riots throughout the southern United States increased as desegregation began to take place. This would cause a shift in the resistance.

Around the time the Civil Rights Act was passed, an up-and-coming boxer was making a case to compete for the heavyweight championship of the world. Cassius Marcellus Clay Jr. was born in Louisville, Kentucky, in 1942. While showing promise as a gifted athlete at an early age, Clay suffered from dyslexia. This limited his abilities to read and write for most of his life, but it would not prevent him from becoming a champion of social justice at an early age. He began an amateur boxing career at the age of thirteen. He would then go on to win several state boxing matches that earned him a trip to the 1960 Olympics where he eventually won the gold medal in the lightweight competition. By 1963, Clay became bigger and stronger, which made him a top contender for the heavyweight boxing title. The following year, he fought and eventually defeated Sonny Liston, who was the current heavyweight champion. This made Clay one of the youngest boxers to become heavyweight champion in U.S. history. After his victory, he taunted the media and other opposers of his brash and outspoken style by declaring that he "shook up the world."[20]

What many people during that time were not privy to was that while he was preparing for his fight against Liston, Clay had developed a friendship with Malcolm X that would change his life forever. Convinced by Malcolm X that white America had stripped him of his true heritage and understanding of his ancestors, Clay changed his name to Cassius X before fully changing his name to Muhammad Ali. He soon revealed that he had also converted to the Muslim faith by joining the Nation of Islam. It was during this time that Ali began to vehemently protest the violence and discriminatory behaviors that Black people had to endure despite the passage of the Civil Rights Act.

As mentioned, the Nation of Islam's ideology was that Black liberation should be met through segregation. This mentality would go on to suggest that the white's man religion, food, and school system were not compatible with the needs and desires of Black Americans. Further, they explained that it was Black Americans' right to protect themselves by any means necessary. Now having the spotlight of being the heavyweight champion, Ali became even more vocal on issues such as religious freedom, inequality, war, and poverty. He especially implored the necessity to respect the name he had chosen and to call out the hypocrisy of America. This would cause him to be one of the most famous and controversial figures of the movement.

The mid-1960s saw the slow decline of the civil rights movement. The Nation of Islam severed ties with Malcolm X due to various conflicts of interest. Because Ali firmly believed in the Nation of Islam, this was also causing a rift between him and Malcolm X. Before they could reconcile, Malcolm X was assassinated in 1965 while giving a speech in the Audubon Ballroom in Harlem, New York. Additionally, the United States was also embroiled in a bitter war with Vietnam. Still, Ali continued to champion social justice issues, much to the chagrin of the U.S. government. To thwart his rise in the movement, the U.S. government decided to draft him into military service so that he could be removed from the media spotlight. The problem with this was that when Ali turned eighteen and was required to sign up for selective military service, he was declared unfit due to his dyslexia.

To work around this, the government decided to lower their standards for military entrance, which subsequently made Ali eligible. However, Ali declared himself a conscientious objector of the war, citing his religious beliefs and opposition to the war. He went on to say,

Man, I ain't got no quarrel with them Viet Cong. . . . Why should they ask me to put on a uniform and go 10,000 miles from home and drop bombs and bullets on brown people in Vietnam while so-called Negro people in Louisville are treated like dogs and denied simple human rights?[21]

On April 28, 1967, Ali arrived in Houston, Texas, for his scheduled induction into the U.S. military. When his name was called, he refused to be sworn in. As a result, he was arrested and subsequently stripped of his heavyweight title. He would go on to be publicly ostracized and ridiculed. However, he held to the Islamic faith, which declares that no man should be involved in aggressive acts unless in self-defense.

Upon hearing this news, a group of other high-profile athletes planned a convention to discuss the best ways to support Ali and to discuss other pressing issues for Black America. Hall of Fame basketball players Bill Russell and Lew Alcindor (later Kareem Abdul-Jabbar) headlined a list of prominent Black athletes in what was called the Cleveland Summit. Convened by Hall of Fame running back Jim Brown, this meeting would also include prominent Cleveland attorney Carl Stokes, members of the Nation of Islam, and boxing promoter Bob Arum. As much as Ali thought the meeting was for coming up with solutions to combat the government and boxing commission, Arum and others tried to get him to compromise by fighting exhibition matches for U.S. troops. This way, the government would drop the charges against him for draft dodging, the boxing commission would reinstate his title, and the proceeds from the fights would go to other Black athletes.

Unconvinced that the compromise would lead to true change, Ali upheld his decision to refuse to fight in the Vietnam War. Consequently, on June 20, 1967, Ali showed up for the trial and was found guilty of violating the Selective Service laws. Although he did not receive jail time, he was banned from boxing. During this ban, Ali gave lectures across the country admonishing war while continuing to speak against the social ills faced by the Black community. Also, society as a whole began to denounce the war. This would further galvanize other prominent Black athletes to use their platform on the global stage.

I'M BLACK AND I'M PROUD

By the late 1960s, the movement had expanded but became erratic in its agenda. Malcolm X had been assassinated. Several resistance organizations such as the Black Panther Party, Mexican American activists, environmentalist regimes, and gay rights organizations all vied for the spotlight. Dr. King, who had given his most famous "I Have a Dream" speech in 1963, was assassinated in 1968. Tensions rose as Black people began to lose hope in a movement that had seemingly jump-started the eradication of inequality for various marginalized groups. However, it was one act of resistance that brought the movement to the global stage.

In 1967, former athlete and noted sociologist Dr. Harry Edwards created the Olympics Project on Human Rights (OPHR) as a way to eradicate racism in the United States and globally. Their initial goal—to boycott the 1968 Olympics—had four demands:

1. South Africa and Rhodesia were to be uninvited from the 1968 Olympic Games due to European colonialism.
2. The New York State Athletic Commission was to restore Ali's heavy-weight boxing title.
3. Avery Brundage, then-president of the International Olympic Committee, must resign immediately.
4. More Black assistant coaches must be hired in U.S. sports.[22]

One of the first major acts of resistance from this organization was showcased one year later during the 1968 Olympic Games.

Prominent Black sprinters Tommie Smith and John Carlos participated in the men's two-hundred-meter relay. Smith and Carlos, who cofounded OPHR with Dr. Edwards, felt compelled to bring the Black plight to the world's stage. Smith won the gold medal and Carlos won the bronze medal, while Australian sprinter Peter Norman won the silver medal. Before receiving their medals, Smith and Carlos planned a series of demonstrations in solidarity with Black Americans. Both athletes arrived at the podium without shoes but wore Black socks to demonstrate solidarity with poverty in Black communities globally. Carlos wore beads to represent Black people who died during the Middle Passage and the survivors who were lynched. Smith wore a Black scarf to showcase pride in being Black in America. But a chance accident would have them go down in global infamy.

Both Smith and Carlos initially planned to bring Black gloves to their event. However, Carlos forgot his at their Olympic Village. Norman, who supported the OPHR, suggested that Smith give his left-handed glove to Carlos. Smith and Carlos agreed and went on to the podiums to accept their medals. At the playing of the U.S. national anthem, Smith raised a clenched right hand, and Carlos raised a clinched left hand to showcase solidarity in the Black plight while all three wore OPHR badges. As global news organizations broadcast the incident, it became known as the Black Power salute. For Black Americans, it was a moment of joy. For Brundage and other white Americans, it represented disrespect to the flag and the country. Because of their actions, Brundage banned them from the games. Norman was not banned. But upon his return home to Australia, he was ostracized by members of the media and the government. For Smith and Carlos, they also returned home to vitriol and hate via the U.S. media. However, many Black Americans considered them heroes and vital to a movement that was waning.

ONE MORE PUSH

Despite landmark decisions such as the Voting Rights Act of 1964 and the Immigration Act of 1965, people were still questioning how much progress had been made regarding racial reconciliation. One athlete continued the fight for equality well beyond the movement. Arthur Ashe was born on July 10, 1943, in Richmond, Virginia.[23] As a child, he was slightly built, which would earn him the nicknames "Skinny" and "Bones." His mother died during his youth, so he was raised by his father. His father, who was a caretaker at a local park, lived on the grounds, which featured several tennis courts. It was here that he would be exposed to the game.

At the age of six, Ashe received training from Dr. R. Walter Johnson who was a noted physician in Virginia. Dr. Johnson, who also coached Althea Gibson years earlier, instilled in Ashe the focus of developing both his athletic skills and his intellectual acumen. Ashe excelled at tennis, eventually earning a full scholarship to UCLA. By his junior year, he had become the first African American player to win U.S. men's hard court championships. During his senior year, he led the NCAA to a national title by winning singles and doubles matches. Upon graduation, Ashe served two years in the military before becoming a professional tennis player in 1969. Heavily influenced by his desire to engage in human rights issues, he found his path when he saw the 1968 Olympic Games protest by Tommie Smith and John Carlos. He would use these ideas to envision a better global society for all.

Throughout the 1960s and 1970s, Ashe garnered several tennis championships, including becoming the first African American male to win singles titles at Wimbledon, the U.S. Open, and the Australian Open. He also helped found the Association of Tennis Professionals, which would become the governing body of men's tennis. Health issues forced Ashe to retire early in 1980, but this would only fuel his activism more. Over the next decade, Ashe protested apartheid in South Africa and pushed for better educational opportunities for all athletes. However, he contracted HIV, which doctors believed happened through a blood transfusion from a prior health issue. This prompted him to become a global ambassador for HIV and AIDS research. Before his death in 1993, he founded the Arthur Ashe Institute for Urban Health and was also named sportsman of the year for *Sports Illustrated*. His legacy for global human rights issues became the last push for athlete activism before its eventual dormancy.

FADE TO BLACK: I AIN'T NO ROLE MODEL

In 1971, the U.S. Supreme Court overturned the initial 1967 trial decision against Ali. The ruling cited that a court of appeals that upheld the initial decision did not attest to why they did not exempt Ali for his conscientious objector stance. That same year, he returned to boxing after being granted a license to fight in Georgia one year earlier. This spawned two fights against boxer Joe Frazier. Ali eventually reclaimed his heavyweight title in 1974 by defeating the then-favorite, George Foreman. In the third match with Frazier the following year, Ali defeated him but was never really the same again. Angelo Dundee, Ali's trainer, felt that Ali could have been more formidable in the boxing world if the U.S. government did not rob him of his prime athletic years. Still, Ali would go on to fight for social justice for the rest of his career and beyond.

But by the early 1970s, the civil rights movement was all but over. The U.S. government began to fight against any resistance movement that challenged its authority. For example, although the Black Panther Party (BPP) was created to challenge police brutality and provide basic needs to the Black community, the government deemed them a terrorist group due to their insistence on remaining armed and monitoring the police in the Oakland Police Department. Moreover, former Federal Bureau of Investigation (FBI) director J. Edgar Hoover declared BPP as "the greatest threat to the internal security of the country."

Additionally, many of the champions for Black liberation during the earlier part of the twentieth century began to pass away. Jackie Robinson, who broke the color barrier in MLB, died in 1972. Paul Robeson, who fought valiantly for Black liberation globally, died a recluse for refusing to denounce his socialist beliefs. At the same time, U.S. sports began to grow in popularity. With this emerging phenomenon, sports broadcast leaders felt the need to take advantage.

The worldwide sports broadcasting leader ESPN (Entertainment and Sports Programming Network) was founded in 1978 and launched its first broadcast in 1979. As ESPN grew, it gained the rights to broadcast live sporting events ranging from college to professional rankings. By the 1980s, more and more athletes were becoming household names. Additionally, the negotiations between sports organizations and broadcasting companies such as ESPN spawned a revenue-sharing program that exponentially increased the earnings of both owners of teams and players. Given this, athletes began to turn away from social causes and focus on increasing their earnings. The sports apparel company Nike believed that attaching their product to popular athletes would be mutually beneficial. With this notion, they signed then-rookie NBA player

Michael Jordan to a deal in which he would get his signature line of shoes for $500,000 per year.[24] This move set the stage for athletes to receive major endorsement deals in addition to increased salaries.

By the 1990s, long gone were the days of athlete activism. Athletes were enjoying their endorsement deals, acting roles, having action figures made in their likeness, and multimillion-dollar contracts. The era of commodification had commenced. Athletes tried their best to stay away from political conversations for fear of losing out on revenue. Still, Black people continued to face issues such as police brutality, an increase in drug use in impoverished communities, and racial profiling. The most infamous issue during that time was the beating of Rodney King at the hands of the Los Angeles Police Department (LAPD) in 1991. One year later, a trial was convened against the officers involved in the incident, but they were eventually acquitted of the charges. Consequently, riots ensued throughout Los Angeles for six days, prompting many Black people to call upon leaders to emerge and speak out against this and other issues.

While some leaders spoke out against the beating, it was not met with the same vigor as leaders during the civil rights era. Relative to athletes speaking out against social issues during that time, some felt it was not their place. One of the more controversial instances of this was NBA Hall of Famer Charles Barkley's 1993 Nike commercial in which he insisted that he was not a role model. He further suggested that he was not paid to be a role model, and instead parents should be role models. He ended the commercial by saying that just because he dunks a basketball, that does not mean he should raise a person's child. While Barkley was trying to suggest that young Black kids should aspire to more than just being an athlete, critics suggested that he was out of touch with the reality that Black children were still not getting the same opportunities to succeed as their white counterparts. Barkley's stance regarding athletes being role models does not negate the fact that some athletes spoke out against social ills. However, the passion and power for these stances were not as bold as those of Ali and others. The relative dormancy of the Black athlete activist would hold fast for almost two more decades. But one particular social movement would help revitalize the athlete activist platform.

Chapter Two

All Lives Matter!
Well, Except . . .

As mentioned previously, athlete activism was in a period of dormancy from the early 1980s to the late 2000s. This dormancy permeated throughout all sports but was noticed more in U.S. professional sports. As athlete activism and its subsequent media coverage waned, the criticisms of Black athlete exploitation grew. The commercialization of Black athletes for the benefit of sports leagues became a point of consternation for Black people, who expressed that this was another example of Black people being used for their labor without the benefits of equitable business practices. No situation seemed more exploitative than that of Black college athletes.

Starting in the late 1980s, many people recognized the increasing popularity of high-revenue-generating college sports such as men's college basketball and football. This was primarily due to the influx of Black college athletes within these sports at predominantly white institutions (PWIs). Just twenty years prior, Black students were having difficulties in attending these universities due to the lag in integration. But Black student-athletes were garnering the attention of PWI coaches. By the 1970s, several Black athletes had infiltrated college sports, though there was still a lag in the Jim Crow South. No situation was more prominent than the coaching habits of then–University of Alabama head football coach Paul "Bear" Bryant.

During this time, Bryant had amassed three college championships and was considered one of the greatest coaches in college football history. But U. W. Clemon, a prominent Black lawyer in Alabama, filed a lawsuit against the university claiming that Bryant purposefully would not give scholarship offers to Black players. The lawsuit became so high profile that then–FBI director J. Edgar Hoover was rumored to have kept tabs on the case as part of the ongoing push against the Civil Rights Act of 1964.

25

On September 12, 1970, the game of college football would change forever as the University of Southern California Trojans football team visited the University of Alabama Crimson Tide football team. The Trojans, which featured a fully integrated football team led by Black running back Sam Cunningham, was the first of its kind to play against the Crimson Tide. The game resulted in a convincing 41–21 victory by the Trojans. In what was likely not a coincidence, soon after the loss, Bryant began recruiting and offering scholarships to Black players. As a result, the lawsuit by Clemon was dropped. Ultimately, the Trojans' victory, coupled with the notoriety of the lawsuit, is often perceived to have led to the integration of football within the southern United States.

As integration flourished throughout college sports, Black student-athletes began to become as popular as professional athletes. Michael Jordan was one of the most high-profile athletes in the United States as a member of the University of North Carolina–Chapel Hill Tar Heels basketball team in 1982. Chris Webber, Juwan Howard, and Jalen Rose were members of arguably the most talented freshman class of basketball players to ever play while on the University of Michigan (Wolverines) basketball team in 1991, and all went on to become NBA stars. Colloquially termed the "Fab Five," they became the first basketball team to make it to the NCAA basketball championship game featuring a team with all freshman starters.

Since that time, the presence of Black athletes in college sports has become synonymous with high-revenue-generating Division I sports. Moreover, most of the athletes who play men's college basketball and men's college football are Black. But the NCAA, which does not allow student-athletes to get paid, earned millions from advertising and broadcasting rights from the popularity of these sports. Therefore, while head coaches were earning millions of dollars a year coaching these athletes, the athletes themselves were often struggling to meet their basic needs. Several critics compared these practices to modern-day slave labor. But considering the dormancy of athlete activism and the fear of losing scholarships, many of these athletes felt powerless.

There have been several critics on either side of the argument relative to the exploitation of Black college athletes. For example, USC professor Shaun Harper wrote a report that explained that Black student-athletes have low graduation rates due to a majority of their time being spent practicing and competing.[1] However, it has also been mentioned that Black student-athletes should not complain, considering the fact that they receive scholarships.[2] Regardless of these conflicting ideas, certain intangibles are provided to these athletes, including openness to diversity, leadership skills, and general life skills. Still, student-athletes' experiences are often different from their nonathlete peers. For example, student-athletes are often advised to take courses that fit around their athletic schedules, which often clash with the courses or majors these students would like to consider. Additionally, the graduation rates of these athletes often fall below their nonathlete peers. Collectively, these incidents have often called into question the validity of the "student" part of the term "student-athlete."

Other than some notable athletes such as former NBA players Etan Thomas and Curt Flood, who are both outspoken critics against racial injustice, athlete activism during the 1990s and early 2000s was largely taboo. The commercialization of sports meant that any idea that created bad press for the business bottom line of sports would be met with swift punishment. Consequently, it became important to understand how any notion of activism would influence perhaps sports' chief stakeholder: the fans.

Scholars George Cunningham and Michael R. Regan Jr. wanted to understand the perception of Black athletes who endorsed certain products based on what type of activism the athlete engaged in.[3] In their study, they found that Black athletes who engaged in activism that was focused on topics such as obesity were perceived more positively than those who focused on more controversial topics such as war. Additionally, those athletes who associated more closely with their ethnic identity were also perceived more negatively than those who did not closely associate with their ethnic identity. These perceptions led to feelings of distrust toward more ethnically identifying athletes and thus provided an avenue for understanding why organizations might choose certain athletes as product endorsers over others.

As such, the 1990s represented a changing of the guard in critical discussions on various social issues. The sports world was no different. During this time, Nike released a popular commercial showcasing the power and resilience of female athletes and the power of sport to empower the masses. Albeit noble, the commercial was criticized for still showing women as needing help instead of being leaders with power.

This left many to believe that the messages representing sport as an agent for social change were weak at best. Over its history, sport has contributed to various social issues including ableism, homophobia, racism, and ageism. More so, sport during this time became a burgeoning tool for socialization and assimilation into American culture.

Along with this, the world was going through an innovation shift as the advent of technology was making the world more interconnected. Email and the internet were changing how we communicate. With these levels of communication, the world became more focused on a democratic process of governing.

In a similar vein, idealists and scholars alike recognized that sport already had a democratic connection given its focus on playing fair, sportsmanship, equal opportunity, and other paths of proper competition. By the 2000s, the idea that sport can be used as a vehicle for social change became evident. More so, the rise of commercialized major global sporting events such as the Olympic Games has illuminated a need to use sport for the betterment of humankind. Further, these concepts have suggested sport as a dissemination medium for pushing forward policy reform on social injustice. Even though the message of sport as a platform for social change was inherently relevant, social injustice persisted.

While the sports world was in its dormancy years in terms of activism, there were still several high-profile incidents that caused national controversy. One example of such an incident occurred on April 4, 2007. Radio host Don Imus was met with scrutiny after he made racially charged comments concerning members of the Rutgers University women's basketball team. In talking with his producer about a game between Rutgers University and the University of Tennessee–Knoxville, Imus began insulting the players by mocking their appearance and eventually calling them "nappy-headed hos."

Outrage ensued as many people called for Imus to be fired. Further, his comments sparked a national conversation regarding the racial stereotypes that denigrate Black Americans for their hair texture. To try to save his job, Imus apologized for his remarks and reiterated that he was a good person that just had an error in judgment. Still, MSNBC and CBS both dropped Imus's show, *Imus in the Morning*, after civil rights leaders Rev. Al Sharpton and Jesse Jackson called for his firing.

However, Imus, along with many of his supporters, claimed that there was a double standard in how racial epithets are used in the media, emphasizing that rap lyrics use similar words all the time to describe women. Further, Imus and his supporters believed that there was an overreaction to his statement and that his career should not be ruined because of it. What would further incite controversy was when a few months after his show was canceled, he signed a five-year, $40 million contract with New York–based radio station WABC. In addition, his namesake program returned to the air within two years of the incident. This furthered the notion among many Black people that their concerns regarding racial discrimination go unheard.

WE HAVE A VOICE TOO

On the night of February 26, 2012, an unarmed Black teenager named Trayvon Martin was walking home from a convenience store carrying a bag of Skittles and a soda. A neighborhood watchman, George Zimmerman, had noticed the teen walking down the street and immediately called the police dispatch. Zimmerman, who claimed to have been noticing several robberies in his community, felt that since the teen was wearing a hood, he looked suspicious. Although the police dispatch warned Zimmerman not to approach the teen, he disregarded the advice and walked over to Martin's vicinity. Zimmerman questioned the teen about his presence in the community, and after an intense argument a scuffle ensued.

As the scuffle continued, Zimmerman was able to pull out his gun and ultimately shot Martin, which fatally wounded him. An uproar followed as media personalities, activists, athletes, and social media users nationwide called out for justice regarding the safety and protection of Black lives. The incident became such a polarizing phenomenon that noted civil rights attorney Benjamin Crump represented Martin's parents in pursuing charges against Zimmerman. The following year, an official trial began as Florida state attorney Angela Corey led the prosecution against Zimmerman. However, after two days of deliberation, the jury found Zimmerman not guilty, supporting his claim that he was acting in self-defense against Martin.

As a result of the verdict, protests took place nationwide calling for national policy reform and the eradication of police brutality against unarmed Black people. Athletes joined in, admonishing the jurors associated with Trayvon's trial by posting tweets in association with Black Lives Matter (BLM). For example, Miami Heat players posted a picture on their Twitter account in which they wore hoodies. This symbolized the attire Trayvon Martin was wearing the night he was killed by Zimmerman. Other players from various sports would also go on to tweet their frustrations with the verdict.

Emboldened by the verdict, activist Alicia Garza wrote a Facebook post admonishing police for their apathy of Black lives. She would further lament that she was surprised at how little Black lives matter and that she would use all of her available resources to sustain Black lives. Her friend, Patrisse Cullors, supported the effort by posting a Twitter hashtag that simply read, #BlackLivesMatter. Recognizing the importance of the statement and the need to develop a sustainable platform for the movement, Garza and Cullors teamed up with activist Opal Tometi to help develop a structure for their platform. The movement gained moderate traction until more instances of police brutality occurred.

As mentioned in chapter 1, athlete activism was virtually nonexistent by the turn of the twenty-first century. Athletes' fears of losing endorsements, a positive public image, and their jobs were the main culprits behind its dormancy. Despite this, instances of police brutality, racial profiling, socioeconomic disparities, and other social ills that plagued marginalized groups continued to increase. The rise of social media and mobile devices further illuminated these issues. Online platforms such as Twitter and Facebook allow users to express their thoughts regarding any topic that comes to mind. Further, these thoughts can be shared either anonymously or without immediate backlash. With millions of followers on these platforms, information can spread quickly. In knowing this, several users have specifically used these platforms to galvanize social change initiatives.

As several social movements such as Black Lives Matter began to establish the voices of those who previously felt powerless in battling racial injustice, the sports world would rise to find their voice as well. Two of the more prominent outlets that arose during BLM are the *Players' Tribune* and *Andscape* (formerly, *The Undefeated*). In 2014, New York Yankee shortstop Derek Jeter was completing his final season as an MLB player. As a five-time World Series champion, Jeter was ready to move on to the next phase of his career as a business mogul and philanthropist. As a high-profile athlete, Jeter noticed the vitriol that athletes faced from the media when it came to scandals or team drama. In wanting to provide a space for athletes to share their varied perspectives, he decided to launch a multimedia platform.

On October 1, 2014, Jeter launched the *Players' Tribune* as a platform that provides daily sports conversations and first-person viewpoints from both professional and college athletes. Several professional athletes from various sports were assigned as senior editors, including Russell Wilson, Danica Patrick, and Blake Griffin. Since its launch, the media platform has dedicated breaking news columns to athletes. For example, several athletes used the website to announce their retirement, including Kobe Bryant and David Ortiz. Some athletes have used the site to discuss their thoughts on racial injustice and other forms of inequity. For instance, Blake Griffin gave an account of his experiences regarding former LA Clippers owner Donald Sterling being banned from the NBA for insensitive language against Black people. Cincinnati Bengals defensive tackle Mike Daniels discussed the importance of Juneteenth, the celebration of the end of slavery, needing to be a federal holiday. In sum, the media platform has provided a consistent avenue for athletes to discuss various topics from retirement status to social injustices.

THE MEDIA'S EFFECT ON SOCIETY

When we chat with friends, watch the latest online streaming series, engage with people at work, or go grocery shopping, intergroup communication is likely to occur. No matter where we choose to live, work, and play, we cannot escape the interactions. What we do have a choice in is how we perceive others based on these interactions. At the summation of these interactions, we inevitably and inextricably develop an "us" versus "them" mentality.

For example, when members of society see megacorporations such as Amazon create monopolies by purchasing other businesses, they might assume that only extraordinarily rich individuals control society. Organizational communication scholar Dr. Stanley Deetz theorized that megacorporations control the very being of society. He further explained that corporations colonize our thoughts, perceptions, and realities. Given this, one of the most powerful entities to construct this notion is media organizations.

A plethora of scholarly inquiries have suggested that consistent exposure to media perpetuates a negative stereotype of individuals from underrepresented groups. Additionally, this type of media exposure has led to decreased support for policy reforms that support issues faced by these same groups. Many of these scholars have suggested that how we assign certain stereotypes to ourselves and others is also perpetuated by constant media exposure. For example, philosopher Marshall McLuhan coined the phrase "The medium is the message."[4] The meaning behind this phrase is that as technology advances, the way we communicate also advances. Consequently, social media platforms such as Twitter and Facebook have allowed prejudice and discrimination to permeate throughout society with relatively little consequence. Communication professor George Gerbner would also coin the phrase "mean world syndrome."[5] Simply put, the mean world syndrome has been widely debated relative to its notion that continued exposure to violence in media creates thoughts of a mean world. A result of this could be the categorization of people into those who are considered violent versus those who are considered wholesome, decent human beings. When considering intergroup relations, people tend to find favor with those who fit their in-group status while remaining skeptical of those who remain outside of their status.

As mentioned, media organizations disproportionately showcase stories that negatively impact improvements in intergroup relations. While much research has shown that positive depictions of racial minorities could lead to these improvements, recent research has suggested that negative media exposure has cultivated a mean world concept that threatens a majority member's idea of a moral and just world. In other words, media exposure has been so negative that the majority members of society may never believe that there are good members of minority groups.

When it comes to understanding media, several theoretical concepts explain how and why we depend on media to determine how we function as a society. Two of the more relevant concepts are cultivation theory and agenda-setting theory.[6] Cultivation theory suggests that overexposure to repetitive messages and themes creates a reality that is often unchallenged by dominant members of society (e.g., white Americans). Agenda-setting theory expresses the notion that the media does not tell a person what to think. Rather, it tells a person what to think about. In other words, repetitive messages will subconsciously establish one's perceptions of society. Taken collectively, these theories explain that media establishes a mean world perception where one's perceptions of victimhood, insecurities, and anxiety are elevated when exposed to excessive violence.

Considering the premise of BLM and intergroup interactions perpetuated in the media, it makes sense that there is tension between those who call out police brutality and others who consider the police as law-abiding individuals who are just working to protect and serve. While media organizations represent several constituencies, one thing remains clear: how stereotypes, prejudices, and other forms of ill thoughts toward underrepresented groups are perpetuated on these platforms will continue to stifle positive intergroup relations.

ATHLETES SPEAK UP

After George Zimmerman's trial, Annelie Schmittel and Jimmy Sanderson examined the reactions of NFL players toward the verdict.[7] First, it was suggested that athletes anticipated a not-guilty verdict through their tweets due to previous media exposure suggesting that when Black people are involved in court-related indictments, they usually receive nonfavorable news. Next, tweets of disbelief were reported, as NFL players believed that the evidence in the Zimmerman trial suggested that Martin was innocent. Third, players tweeted their frustrations with the American justice system. They suggested substantial reforms that would eradicate the unfairness of verdicts that go against Black people. Fourth, players suggested that the ethics and morals of American society took a blow and remained emblematic of racial inequities that continue to predominate. Lastly, players sent their condolences to the Martin family while also empathizing with the pain of losing their son. Despite this, several high-profile shootings would follow.

In 2014, a slew of police-related deaths manifested. First, New York resident Eric Garner was choked to death by police officers after being arrested. As police pinned him down, Garner could be heard saying, "I can't breathe." Next, Ferguson, Missouri, teen Michael Brown was gunned down by a police officer after speculation that had he robbed a convenience store. Eyewitnesses explained that Brown was left in the street for over four hours after he was fatally wounded.

Finally, twelve-year-old Cleveland resident Tamir Rice was gunned down by police after a dispatch call described a male pointing a gun at residents in a local park. During the dispatch, the accuser speculated that the gun was fake and that the perpetrator was most likely a juvenile. Immediately after arriving at the scene, a police officer shot Rice in the torso. He was rushed to the hospital where he eventually died. Upon review, the gun that Rice was holding was discovered to be fake. In all instances, the police officers were either not indicted or were acquitted of the charges levied against them.

Outrage and protests from these instances prompted several social media users to post "#BlackLivesMatter" in solidarity with friends and family who had had negative altercations with law enforcement. As the movement gained momentum, the mission flourished under several premises: the eradication of police brutality against Black and brown people, the liberation of all Black people and others who are marginalized, and a world free of systematic oppression.

BANNED FOR LIFE

While the BLM movement was finding its footing on the national stage, another sports scandal put into question the continued struggle for racial reconciliation. On April 25, 2014, an audio recording of LA Clippers owner Donald Sterling and his mistress, V. Stiviano, was released by the media outlet TMZ. In the recording, Sterling was heard arguing with Stiviano regarding an Instagram photo in which she is seen posing with former NBA player Magic Johnson. Specifically, he said,

> It bothers me a lot that you want to broadcast that you're associating with Black people. . . . You can sleep with [Black people]. You can bring them in, you can do whatever you want. . . . The little I ask you is . . . not to bring them to my games.[8]

Upon hearing this, several athletes, sports team leaders, and others spoke out against Sterling. For example, Kareem Abdul-Jabbar, Shaquille O'Neal, Michael Jordan, and other NBA players condemned Sterling. Miami Heat owner Micky Arison would express that there was no room for Sterling in the NBA. Also, Virgin America, CarMax, and several other organizations would end their sponsorship deals with the team. Additionally, President Obama would express regret with Sterling's statements by calling them highly offensive.

A few days after the audio was released, NBA commissioner Adam Silver said that Sterling would be banned for life and fined him a league constitutional maximum of $2.5 million. Additionally, Silver immediately began the transition of putting the team up for sale. Sterling eventually agreed to the ban and sold the team for $2 billion to former Microsoft CEO Steve Ballmer. This move represented one of the first maximum-level punishments within the sport that dealt with racial injustice. The topic of racial reconciliation under the lens of BLM was still in its infancy.

HANDS UP, DON'T SHOOT!

As the reputation of the BLM movement grew as a formidable opponent against social injustice, so did the activism of athletes. On November 29, 2014, members of the Knox College women's basketball team garnered national attention for their show of solidarity toward the Michael Brown shooting.[9] Particularly, Ariyana Smith walked onto her team's basketball court with her hands raised and fell to the floor where she remained for four and a half minutes. This demonstration was symbolic of the four and a half hours that Brown lay slain on the ground. The following day, five St. Louis Rams (now Los Angeles Rams) players decided to engage in a pregame demonstration that showcased their disdain against the shooting of Brown.[10] The players, which included Tavon Austin, Stedman Bailey, Chris Givens, Kenny Britt, and Jared Cook, entered the field by holding their hands up in a way that suggested their surrender to the police. The pregame gesture, which symbolized a nationwide movement primarily by Black men to relay a message of not wanting to get shot by law enforcement, represented one of the first modern-day sport gestures that exclusively called out the police for brutality-related issues. It also drew the ire of local law enforcement.

The St. Louis Police Officers' Association (SLPOA) was angered at the demonstration. They said that the players acted out of ignorance and that they ignored all of the evidence that suggested the officer involved in the shooting operated within proper police procedure. Further, they released an official statement saying that the organization was "profoundly disappointed with the members of the St. Louis Rams football team who chose to ignore the mountains of evidence released from the St. Louis County Grand Jury this week and engage in a display that police officers around the nation found tasteless, offensive, and inflammatory."[11]

Then–Rams coach Jeff Fisher and other team administrators claimed that they were unaware of the players' plans for a demonstration. However, they supported the players' freedom of speech. The SLPOA doubled down on their anger against the Rams players by requesting that the NFL punish the demonstrators. League officials decided not to punish the players because of a long-standing common practice of not punishing players for political gestures. NFL spokesperson Brian McCarthy said, "We respect and understand the concerns of all individuals who have expressed views on this tragic situation."[12]

A few days later, then–Cleveland Cavalier player LeBron James showed up in a pregame warm-up with an "I Can't Breathe" T-shirt as a symbolic gesture to the deaths of Garner and others.[13] Los Angeles Lakers star Kobe Bryant and other members of the team followed suit by wearing similar T-shirts. Soon, several members of the NBA began to wear the shirt. In the NFL, then–Cleveland Browns receiver Andrew Hawkins would don a T-shirt that read "Justice for Tamir Rice—John Crawford" on the front and "The Real Battle of Ohio" on the back. Crawford, who was also shot and killed by police at a Walmart in Ohio, represented the latest in a seemingly nationwide epidemic of law enforcement–related deaths.

Similar to the outrage by Missouri officers, the Cleveland Police Union (CPU) also expressed their anger toward the NFL. In a statement released by a CPU spokesperson, they said, "It's pretty pathetic when athletes think they know the law. They should stick to what they know best on the field. The Cleveland Police protect and serve the Browns stadium, and the Browns organization owes us an apology."[14] In a subsequent statement, the Browns organization said,

> We have great respect for the Cleveland Police Department and the work that they do to protect and serve our city. We also respect our players' rights to project their support and bring awareness to issues that are important to them if done so in a responsible manner.[15]

While support for the BLM movement was growing among athletes and nonathletes alike, detractors of the movement took to social media by posting "#AllLivesMatter" and "#BlueLivesMatter" to counter what they perceived as a movement that sought to eliminate police and center Black people as the only lives that are important. Both movements became popularized after two New York police officers were shot and killed in retaliation for the Eric Garner and Michael Brown deaths at the hands of police earlier that year. Still, #AllLivesMatter would rise to become the more dominant resistance against the movement. BLM supporters went on to explain that Black lives are not more important than the lives of others. Rather, they said that Black lives should be of equal importance to the lives of others.

While being dubbed the unofficial "new civil rights movement,"[16] BLM has received staunch criticism, from being perceived as a socialist movement to its perceived lack of organizational structure and purpose. What the movement is and what it is not has been up for much debate.

WHAT IS IT?

Since its origins, political pundits, celebrities, the media, and everyday citizens have spent time dissecting the BLM movement, its purpose, and its effectiveness. Some have even suggested that BLM is a terrorist organization that hurts the Black community more than it helps. Despite this, the movement has emerged as a place of intellectual inquiry. For example, a 2017 article examined police brutality incidents that are reported by major and local news outlets close to where the incidents took place.[17] Specifically, they found that both news outlets were sympathetic in their coverage of police brutality against Black people—which is often not the case. They further explained that BLM movement protesters may have influenced news outlets to be more sympathetic to social justice issues than in times past. Contrarily, a 2019 article found that cable news outlets such as Fox News denounce BLM as an organization that uses racism as an excuse to blame white people for their issues.[18]

Still, BLM has transcended from being only an organization that focuses on police brutality. Rather, BLM has risen to be a catalyst for situations such as incarcerated individuals entering back into society. Further, it has been suggested that BLM can establish a new lens through which decision-makers can engage in policy reform regarding wrongful or unusually lengthy imprisonment. Furthermore, some political scientists have even suggested that BLM can serve as a scholarly platform to challenge the future of American democracy. Their thoughts are guided by the following question,

> Can contemporary structures and strictures of American democracy be reformulated to create a future in which African Americans have access to substantive and meaningful forms of economic, political, and social equality?[19]

Simply put, how can BLM become a movement that tangibly engages in policy reform? As scholars on race relations have found that most policies benefit whites while traumatizing Blacks, the answers may lie in a psychological notion that suggests that you "reap what you sow."

BELIEF IN A JUST WORLD

Presumably, people tend to believe that they live in a world with mostly good people. They believe that most people wake up in the morning, get ready for their day, drop their children off at school, go to work, come home, unwind, tuck the children in, and go to sleep. Rinse and repeat. If there is any negative variation in this process, it is typically that person's fault. This concept is called the "belief in a just world" (BJW). Coined by psychologist Melvin J. Lerner, BJW specifically suggests that most people believe that we live in a just world.[20] When it comes to applying for a job, purchasing a home, providing children with proper education, or staying safe, BJW says that people will often do the right things to obtain a successful life. Ultimately, people will get what they deserve.

Within this concept is also the notion of victim blaming. If a person gets caught up in a negative situation, then those who agree with BJW cope by accusing the victim of putting themselves in the situation rather than believing there is corruption in the world. Since its inception, several scholars have studied BJW and its association with victim blaming. For example, one scholar found that rape survivors who speak out about their experience are often chastised by family and friends because they believe that ultimately you reap what you sow. The negative consequence of this is that these responses often silence rape survivors from further disclosing their experiences to others. In another study, a scholar found that poor individuals are often blamed for their misfortune. Relative to a person's BJW, it is often threatened when an innocent person becomes a victim. This thought process usually leads to one's ideas of the world being violated, which often causes increased distress. Therefore, it is more than likely that a person who has high levels of BJW will work to reestablish their beliefs by any means necessary.

One of the most threatening phenomena to one's BJW is race relations in America. For example, scholars found that when a threat to one's BJW is closely associated with someone from their ethnic group, their self-esteem decreases.[21] On the contrary, when a threat to one's BJW is not associated with someone from their own ethnicity, their self-esteem usually remains intact. The researchers would go on to say that people who constantly face threats of injustice in their daily lives not only have decreased self-esteem, but it also decreases their mental and physical well-being along with negatively affecting their personal and professional success opportunities. Given this, race relations and one's BJW often negatively affect individuals from marginalized groups. Much of this tension is caused by what is considered a white racial frame. The concept suggests that white people have a global view that includes notions of negative stereotypes, thoughts, emotions, and actions toward people of color while promoting whiteness as a notion of racial superiority over others.

According to Dr. Lerner, most people believe that social systems regarding human behavior are fair and balanced. Furthermore, he explained that people often view victims of situations that are beyond the scope of the social system as being to blame for their folly, a thought process known as the just world mentality. However, such a mentality "may undermine a commitment to justice."[22]

WILL WE EVER GET ALONG?

There has been a long and destructive history regarding the interactions of Black people and the police. As mentioned in chapter 1, the Jim Crow era witnessed the height of these sordid interactions, so much so that Black parents were forced to engage in survival tactics that often led to instances of shame and inferiority. One of these tactics was what Hazel Erby described as "the talk," a mechanism formalized by Black parents in the late 1940s to tell their children about the harsh realities of being Black in the southern United States.

Initially described in journalist Ray Sprigle's book *In the Land of Jim Crow*, Black parents were observed in conversation providing intricately developed plans for their children to escape instances of police interaction, white-Black interactions, and other racial interactions that were seemingly threatening to their survival.[23] In a deeper explanation of this mechanism, Erby gave an exemplar account of such talks by telling the stories of two prominent figures during that time: Medgar Evers and Emmett Till.

Although Evers and Till could be considered martyrs for the civil rights movement, "the talk" has continued to be a tactic used by Black people to quell racial violence and injustice against their children and other members of the community. Media polarization and the advent of technological advancements represent the next phase of how racial violence and the Black community continue to be a dominant narrative in today's society.

The disdain of police also made its way into the hip-hop world when rap group N.W.A released their controversial song "Fuck the Police."[24] This song was a representation of the frustration that the Black community had toward the police for their hostile tendencies. Scholar Amanda Nell Edgar also explained that the song represented disdain for neoliberalism, which hastened calls for police reform and other social justice movements that stifled the growth of marginalized communities. Lastly, he explained that social media, explicitly YouTube, served as a vital tool to showcase N.W.A's song as a form of social resistance that put control back into the hands of the people.

THE OBJECTION TO BLM

In understanding the premise of BJW and media cultivation, it makes sense that Black people express psychological and physical distress when dealing with white people. This is not to say that all Black people are afraid of white people, nor does it mean that all white people operate in the white racial frame, but it makes sense that much of the conversation of U.S. race relations is one where negative situations are usually blamed on marginalized individuals. Moreover, objectors to BLM may perceive the world as just and instances of police brutality as the victims' fault. As mentioned, supporters of BLM say that Black lives are not more important than any other life. Rather, Black lives should be considered as important as other lives. While All Lives Matter (ALM) supporters say that all lives are important and equal, their perceptions skew toward a notion that BLM is a racist movement. While it is true that all lives should matter, BLM supporters suggest that not all lives face the same instances of racial injustice.

Regardless of the backlash, BLM has grown since its early days of ending police brutality. It has now become a major platform that seeks to make a political stamp on policy reform that liberates Black people and other marginalized groups from a seemingly oppressive socioeconomic status. Consequently, the movement has galvanized a new era of sports activism that focuses on collaborative efforts to create tangible social change.

During the launch of the *Players' Tribune* in 2014, ESPN began developing an online media platform "that will provide in-depth coverage, commentary, and insight on sports, race, and culture directed towards the African-American audience."[25] Then–ESPN columnist Jason Whitlock was tapped to lead the launch of this new media venture. Whitlock would name the online website *The Undefeated* as an homage to the late poet and civil rights leader Maya Angelou when she said, "You may encounter many defeats, but you must not be defeated."

Upon Whitlock's departure from the network, ESPN hired former *Washington Post* managing editor Kevin Merida as editor in chief of the website. Eventually *The Undefeated* would launch on May 17, 2016, as one of a few major media platforms intersecting the areas of race, culture, and sport. In one of the more surprising moves made via the website, Michael Jordan would announce his commitment to helping eradicate social injustice, for which he was previously criticized throughout the entirety of his career for evading the political realm.

In his statement, he would say,

Over the past three decades, I have seen up close the dedication of the law enforcement officers who protect me and my family. I have the greatest respect for their sacrifice and service. I also recognize that for many people of color their experiences with law enforcement have been different than mine. I have decided to speak out in the hope that we can come together as Americans, and through peaceful dialogue and education, achieve constructive change.[26]

To cement his commitment to social justice, Jordan explained that he would donate a total of $2 million to two organizations. The first organization to receive $1 million was the International Association of Chiefs of Police. This association established an Institute for Community-Police Relations dedicated to resolving the disconnect between urban communities and local law enforcement. The second organization to receive a $1 million donation was the NAACP legal defense fund. The defense fund serves as a legal outreach entity that aids people of color with litigation, advocacy, policy research, and scholarship opportunities for Black students.

To further engage the intersection of sport and politics, *The Undefeated* hosted a town hall on October 11, 2016, with former president Barack Obama titled "A Conversation with the President: Sports, Race, and Achievement" on the campus of North Carolina A&T. Led by ESPN anchor Stan Verrett, the town hall focused on the success and challenges remaining in using sports as a platform to engage in tangible social change. Students, faculty, and other attendees were able to engage President Obama with their concerns. Given these scenarios, it showcased the media's burgeoning push to recognize the intelligence, influence, and impact of world-class athletes who also work to eradicate social injustice.

AMATEURS HAVE RIGHTS TOO

College athletes are usually held to stricter standards than professional athletes due to rules and regulations established by both their host institutions and the National College Athletic Association (NCAA), the main governing body of college sports. College athletes, who earn millions of dollars for their institutions and the NCAA, were restricted from partaking in these earnings by their amateur status. Any violation of this would result in them forfeiting their rights to play.

Particularly, high-revenue-generating sports such as NCAA college football and basketball earn these institutions the vast majority of their revenue. As many of the athletes who participate in these high-revenue-generating sports are predominantly African American, critics denounced these institutions by expressing that they earned these wages off the free labor provided by Black athletes. Furthermore, critics interpreted the NCAA's prohibition against paying athletes as racist and discriminatory, a further challenge to the governing body.

Since the BLM movement began, professional athletes have gained momentum in the movement to eradicate social injustice. While some college athletes were participating in demonstrations, many may have felt intimidated to push for procedural change. However, these groups of athletes began to recognize the BLM movement's power in engaging in larger conversations on basic human rights. One group of college athletes, in particular, took this challenge head-on.

At the University of Missouri–Columbia (Mizzou), several undergraduate students spent years pointing out racial injustice both on and off campus. A collective of Black students began to notice that many of their concerns were being ignored by campus administration. Therefore, they formed a coalition called Concerned Student 1950 (CS1950) as a racial injustice strategic initiative.[27] The name CS1950 is an outgrowth of the year the first Black student was admitted to the university.

The 2015 football season proved to be a pivotal moment to the CS1950 as a slew of high-profile police shootings and their continued protests regarding racialized incidents on campus caught the attention of Mizzou football team members. Members of CS1950 camped out in tents on the college campus demanding that then–university president Timothy Wolfe meet with them to hear their concerns. As members of the football team were passing by the encampment, they convened with the CS1950 to discuss what they could do to assist in the protest.

Members of CS1950 said that Wolfe did not grasp the magnitude of racial incidents that affected Black students on campus. For example, they said that Black students would have the N-word yelled at them by passersby. In another incident, Black students found a swastika symbol written in excrement on a campus bathroom wall. When they were finally able to have a sit-down with Wolfe, they believed that their concerns were largely ignored. Consequently, several football players engaged with the larger student community in the campus's Black Cultural Center to discuss how to hold university administration accountable for seemingly ignoring Black student well-being. The result of the meeting was to forfeit their upcoming football games until their list of demands was met.

The players informed their head coach, Gary Pinkel, of what they were wanting to do. He showed support to his players and encouraged them to state their list of demands. Collectively, the students and student-athletes issued eight demands, which were as follows:

1. We demand that University of Missouri System President, Tim Wolfe, write a hand-written apology to Concerned Student 1-9-5-0 demonstrators and hold a press conference in the Mizzou Student Center reading the letter.
2. We demand the immediate removal of Tim Wolfe as UM system president.
3. We demand that the University of Missouri meets the Legions of Black Collegians' demands that were presented in 1969 for the betterment of the Black community.
4. We demand that the University of Missouri creates and enforces comprehensive racial awareness and inclusion curriculum throughout all campus departments and units, mandatory for all students, faculty, staff, and administration.
5. We demand that by the academic year 2017–2018, the University of Missouri increases the percentage of Black faculty and staff members campus-wide by 10 percent.
6. We demand that the University of Missouri composes a strategic 10-year plan on May 1, 2016, that will increase retention rates for marginalized students, sustain diversity curriculum and training, and promote a more safe and inclusive campus.
7. We demand that the University of Missouri increases funding and resources for the University of Missouri Counseling Center to hire additional mental health professionals, particularly those of color, boosting mental health outreach and programming across campus, increasing campus-wide awareness and visibility of the counseling center, and reducing lengthy wait times for prospective clients.
8. We demand that the University of Missouri increases funding, resources, and personnel for the social justice center on campus to hire additional professionals, particularly those of color, boost outreach and programming across campus, and increase campus-wide awareness and visibility.[28]

While many of the terms in the list of demands were more long-term, the immediate effect was that Wolfe resigned as president. Players and students were praised for their efforts in being one of the first nationwide protests that impacted protocols for racialized incidents. Then–president Barack Obama especially praised the athletes for their courage but cautioned for open dialogue between administrators and students. State lawmakers criticized the students, athletes, and supporters of the protest. They proposed a bill called House Bill 1743, which would have stripped scholarships from student-athletes for protesting if passed.[29]

The bill was officially withdrawn, but it still drew criticisms that relegated even the thought of such a bill as antiquated and archaic. Further, critics expressed that anything similar to the notion of stripping scholarships would prevent future student-athletes from exercising their First Amendment rights. While the protests were initially started by students, the student-athletes believed that they could expedite reform due to the university potentially losing millions of dollars because of forfeited games. Conceivably, the university system would agree. The Mizzou athlete protests were one of several high-profile encounters that intersected with the BLM movement. While 2015 saw an increased presence in athlete statements and demonstrations, it was the following year that formally solidified the intersection of the BLM movement and athlete activism.

Chapter Three

United We Stand, Divided We Kneel

Despite mixed reactions regarding the origin and purpose of the Black Lives Matter (BLM) movement, it grew in notoriety. Supporters praised the movement as one that could bring lasting change to the ongoing racist and discriminatory acts that permeated throughout the United States. Detractors continued to challenge the movement by calling it divisive and unnecessary, as claims of Black-on-Black crime were deemed worse than any other crime against Black lives. Still, by 2015, BLM had a formal structure and began to lay out strategic initiatives targeting policy reform.

During that same year, however, outcry regarding police brutality against African Americans ran rampant due to the death of Maryland resident Freddie Gray. On April 12, 2015, Gray was arrested by six Baltimore police on claims that he fled from their presence while in possession of an illegal knife. He was placed in the back of a police van to be taken to the police station. While in transport, Gray suffered a severe spinal injury and was subsequently rushed to the R Adams Cowley Shock Trauma Center within the city. While at the center, it was reported that Gray suffered from an 80 percent severed neck, a few fractured vertebrae, and other injuries, including one to his voice box. After slipping in and out of a coma over the course of a week, Gray succumbed to his injuries. Upon the news of Gray's death, protests ensued throughout Baltimore calling for the arrest and prosecution of the six officers who held Gray in custody.

In their initial report, the six officers associated with the arrest and subsequent death of Gray reported that their presence in his neighborhood was due to State's Attorney Marilyn J. Mosby's mandate to have increased patrol in the area due to high crime. As they patrolled the area, Gray noticed their presence and fled, which ultimately led to his arrest. They then claimed that while en route to their destination, Gray suffered the injuries that ultimately led to his death. However, eyewitness reports and videos showed Gray screaming and being dragged during the arrest procedures before being assisted into the back of the van. Some even reported that he was beaten with a baton before being placed in the van. Regardless, the officers involved were suspended with pay while the incident was investigated.

During this time, the residents of Baltimore engaged in peaceful protests outside the city's police department. But as the official investigation continued, residents became impatient, due in large part to the national belief that officers who kill unarmed Black men are usually acquitted after investigations that claim they followed proper police procedure. As a result, violence ensued as protesters threw rocks, set fires, and destroyed police cars. From this, the sports world began to take further aim at police brutality.

BASEBALL, BASKETBALL, AND BLM

As the city of Baltimore began to get attention from both Freddie Gray's death at the hands of police and the ensuing protests, chants of "Black Lives Matter" began to grow nationwide. The BLM organization showed its support in the initial protests in front of the Baltimore Police Department while recognizing that the violence of the protests was a result of outrage against constant police brutality. Again, the nation either blamed or praised the BLM movement for its role in instigating protests against police officers. But it was the world of sport that was able to continuously provide perspective.

During the Baltimore protests, several individuals from the Baltimore Orioles baseball organization spoke up about the overall issue of police violence and protest. For example, former first baseman Chris Davis explained that the people who were protesting had a right to be upset at the consistent violence against Black and brown people while also calling for there to be peace. Also, former manager Buck Showalter expressed that it was hard to concentrate on playing the game of baseball while violence against Black and brown people persisted. The current CEO of the Orioles, John P. Angeles, who served as chief operating officer of the baseball franchise during this time, tweeted his frustration with those who denounced the protest by saying that the nation must observe the protest as a symptom of a much larger problem of people within Baltimore and around the world whose lives are cut short due to violence. More so, he expressed sympathy for those who continue to suffer while struggling to obtain civil rights. Still, the protests resumed, which prompted other sports figures to step forward.

As mentioned in chapter 2, NBA superstars LeBron James, Carmelo Anthony, Chris Paul, and Dwayne Wade used the ESPY Awards platform to denounce police brutality and other violence against Black and brown Americans. In noticing the national attention the Baltimore protests were receiving, Anthony, who spent much of his youth as a resident of the city, decided to intervene. While a member of the New York Knicks basketball organization at this time, Anthony arrived in Baltimore to march in solidarity with the protesters. With this act, he wanted to show support while also denouncing the violence that was wreaking havoc on the community. He explained that he understood that the community had grown tired of the consistent violence against Black and brown people, but he said that laws and policies cannot be changed overnight. Lastly, he expressed that destroying the community would not aid in the fight for social justice.

Despite his efforts, the violence of the protests continued, so much so that the Baltimore mayor instituted a curfew while also calling in the National Guard to help keep communities safe. Consequently, at least twenty other protests took place in other major cities, including Chicago, Miami, and Philadelphia. The purpose of these subsequent protests was to implore local and federal governments, police departments, and society at large that Black lives should matter as much as other lives. Back in Baltimore, the National Guard was able to quell the violence a few days after Freddie Gray's funeral, and the curfew was lifted. While federal, state, and local governments became aware of the consequences of seemingly unimpeded disregard for Black life at the hands of police, it was another protest that aimed for the symbolism this country was built on that ushered sport to the forefront of the BLM movement.

SITTING TO TAKE A STAND

Following the Baltimore protests, several other high-profile deaths involving Black people and the police occurred. For instance, Texas native Sandra Bland was found hanging in her jail cell from an alleged suicide attempt three days after being arrested for a traffic stop. Her death, which occurred months after Freddie Gray's, garnered national attention. However, BLM leaders expressed that before Bland's death, most cases of violence involving police and Black women went largely ignored by mainstream media. As such, Bland's death was the unfortunate catalyst to a national conversation regarding the protection of Black women and men.

The following year, two other high-profile incidents occurred. First, Louisiana native Alton Sterling was gunned down by police after a response to an altercation behind a local shop. The following day, Minnesota native Philando Castile was shot by police during a routine traffic stop. Castile, who was licensed to carry, informed the officer that he had a firearm in his car. The officer warned him not to reach for the gun. Castile then replied that he was only reaching for his license and registration. Despite this, the officer opened fire, fatally wounding Castile. Once again, national protests ensued calling for the end of police brutality. Micah Johnson, a former army reserve Afghan War veteran, decided to take matters into his own hands when he ambushed and killed five police officers in Dallas, Texas, in retaliation for the murders of Sterling and Castile. Johnson was eventually killed by police officers, but the incident was purportedly described as the deadliest attack on U.S. law enforcement since the September 11, 2001, attacks. The results of these incidents sparked protests calling for both the protection of Black lives and those of police officers.

While this was going on, local citizens, celebrities, sports leaders, and members of the BLM movement were lending their voices to end police brutality. Particularly, they were calling for the officers involved in these shootings to be held responsible for their actions. Up to that point, many of the officers involved in these incidents were either acquitted of all charges brought against them or suspended with pay, but none were found guilty. To some, this lack of accountability had reached a breaking point. For one athlete, the reaction to his frustrations challenged the very fabric this country was built on.

The 2016 NFL season began with its usual preseason games before the start of the regular season. During one of the preseason games, media outlets began to notice that then–San Francisco 49ers quarterback Colin Kaepernick sat on the bench while his teammates and coaches stood during the playing of the national anthem. But it was during a preseason home game against the Green Bay Packers on August 26, 2016, that Kaepernick began to receive national attention for sitting during the celebration of the national anthem. In explaining his reasons, Kaepernick said,

> I am not going to stand up to show pride in a flag for a country that oppresses Blacks and people of color. To me, this is bigger than football and it would be selfish on my part to look the other way. There are bodies in the street and people getting paid leave and getting away with murder.[1]

In response to Kaepernick's protest, the 49ers organization expressed that the national anthem will always represent the freedoms of this country and that individuals have the right to choose whether or not to participate in the pregame anthem ceremony. Likewise, the NFL explained that "players are encouraged but not required to stand during the playing of the national anthem."[2]

THE KNEEL HEARD 'ROUND THE WORLD

In response to Kaepernick's stance, an open letter was penned to him by former NFL long snapper and U.S. Army Green Beret Nate Boyer. In his letter, he described his experiences in global warfare while also acknowledging that racism still exists in the United States. While he one day hoped that Kaepernick would once again stand for the national anthem, he respected his choice to fight against racial injustice and violence in America. He ended the letter by remaining optimistic that society would change.

The following day, Kaepernick, teammate and supporter Eric Reid, and Boyer met to discuss ways that would both show respect to the men and women who serve in the military while also addressing racial injustice. Boyer's position stemmed from the notion that the flag symbolizes freedom and sacrifice. He went on to explain that one of his fellow military members, who died while in service, was brought home draped in the U.S. flag. However, Kaepernick explained that the anthem's notion of liberty and justice for all was lacking when it came to Black and brown people. In working toward a compromise, Kaepernick asked Boyer what would be the best solution to satisfy both sides of the argument. Boyer suggested that kneeling would be a better sign of respect than sitting. Kaepernick and Reid agreed to this and promised that from their meeting onward, they would kneel instead of sitting during the playing of the national anthem.

TO PROTECT AND SERVE OUR IMAGE

Following Kaepernick's continued protest of the national anthem, the Santa Clara Police Officers' Association wrote a letter to the 49ers organization calling for them to engage in immediate disciplinary action. They explained that if the team did not discipline him, they would boycott working to protect and serve at future games. They went on to explain that Kaepernick's actions were misinformed and did not accurately portray the hard work that goes into being a police officer. Given that local law enforcement usually works at major sporting events as a way to protect both fans and players, this statement represented one of the first threats against the working relationship between sports organizations and law enforcement.

Santa Clara police chief Michael Sellers responded to the letter by vowing to continue to have officers work the games. Despite vehemently disagreeing with Kaepernick's stance, Sellers explained that everyone has freedom of speech that is protected under the Constitution, whether one agrees or not. He went on to say that the safety of 49ers patrons was more important than fighting against defamation. But the fight against Kaepernick's protest would not stop there.

The disagreement between Kaepernick and law enforcement gained national prominence when the National Association of Police Organizations became involved. When the executive director of the organization, Bill Johnson, heard that Kaepernick was wearing socks that displayed pigs in police officer hats during training camp, he took his frustrations out on the NFL front office. In his complaint, he explained that the league was showing a double standard when they allowed Kaepernick to continue his protest while teams such as the Dallas Cowboys were not allowed to honor the slain officers who were killed in retaliation to deaths of Freddie Gray and Sandra Bland. Lastly, he admonished the league for failing to protect the public interest by allowing the protest against them.

I STAND WITH KAP

While the 49ers and the NFL were busy trying to determine best practices in handling the anthem protest, league-wide support in solidarity with Kaepernick revealed itself. First, members of the Miami Dolphins franchise, including running back Arian Foster, wide receiver Kenny Stills, and safety Michael Thomas, all kneeled during the national anthem during a regular-season game. As this was the anniversary of the September 11 attacks on the United States, this action forced the Dolphins organization to release a statement encouraging its team members to stand for the anthem but also respecting their freedom of expression.[3] The Seattle Seahawks, who were the opponents of the Dolphins that day, engaged in an alternative gesture by locking arms in unity while standing for the national anthem.

That same day, other players from around the league engaged in alternative gestures in support of Kaepernick. The Kansas City Chiefs' cornerback Marcus Peters raised his fist during the national anthem in solidarity. New England Patriots tight end Martellus Bennett and current safety Devin McCourty also raised their fists during the anthem. The raised fist gesture was in solidarity with former Olympians John Carlos and Tommie Smith, who raised their fists in protest against U.S. racial injustice during the medal ceremony at the 1968 Olympic Games. Soon after, athletes from other sports and at various levels were all showing solidarity toward Kaepernick by either speaking out on or demonstrating against racial and social injustice.

During a National Women's Soccer League match between Seattle Reign and the Chicago Red Stars, Reign star Megan Rapinoe knelt at the playing of the national anthem in support of Kaepernick. She explained that since she was a gay American, she also knew how it felt to not have the U.S. flag represent your full civil liberties. She finished by urging white people to support people of color during a time of national uproar. Next, players and coaches from James A. Garfield High School in Seattle, Washington, knelt during the playing of the national anthem. Head coach Joey Thomas explained that while there may be a disagreement regarding the protest, the larger issue is resolving the issues that people are kneeling for in the first place. The WNBA joined in solidarity as all members of the Indiana Fever and two members of the Phoenix Mercury knelt for the playing of the anthem during the first game of the play-offs.

Kaepernick's influence even went beyond the sports world as several prominent civil rights organizations expressed their support. The NAACP, one of the oldest civil rights organizations in the world, gave their full support to Kaepernick's protest. Leaders of Black Lives Matter also placed their full endorsement behind Kaepernick. Marc Morial, president of the National Urban League, would describe Kaepernick's protest as an act of patriotism.

These sentiments were shared by *Time* magazine executives as they gave Kaepernick the feature of their October 3, 2016, issue. Titled "The Perilous Fight," the magazine explained that Kaepernick's protest fueled a more in-depth national conversation on the intersections of privilege, pride, and patriotism. As the protests continued to gain traction across the country, everyday citizens had different opinions.

While athletes from across the country were standing in solidarity with Kaepernick, media outlets began investigating what everyday citizens thought about the burgeoning protests. In a 2016 Reuters study, 2,093 adults from across the United States, with more than 70 percent of them identifying as white, completed a poll concerning their thoughts on the anthem protest.[4] The results showed that 61 percent of the people polled said they disagreed with Kaepernick. Moreover, 72 percent of Americans said they thought the protest against the national anthem was unpatriotic. However, 64 percent of adults declared that Kaepernick had every right to engage in protest, as this was his freedom of expression. Lastly, 46 percent of adults polled said the NFL should not be penalized or held responsible for the protests.

While common citizens were varied in their support for the anthem protests, several members of the military spoke up regarding Kaepernick's stance. In an open letter featured on ESPN's sport and pop culture website *The Undefeated*, thirty-five military veterans from various ethnic and gender backgrounds showed an overwhelming amount of support. In the letter, they expressed that they commend all athletes from Jackie Robinson to Colin Kaepernick who challenge racism and other forms of discrimination that have permeated the American landscape.

Additionally, they went on to admonish those who fought against the Black Lives Matter movement. Further, they expressed that Kaepernick's kneeling was not a sign of disrespect to them. Rather, it was an expression of their sacrifice for every American to have the right to freedom of speech. Lastly, they explained that athletes and everyday citizens who actively seek justice in society are showing the highest form of patriotism. Still, disagreements across ethnicity, political affiliation, and other societal demographics regarding whether the anthem protests were anti-American persisted. What many were not expecting was that this protest would make it into the presidential conversation.

PRESIDENTIAL PENALTY

By the end of the 2016 NFL season, the United States found itself in political disarray. President Barack Obama was in the last year of his presidential term. Presidential candidates Donald Trump and Hillary Clinton were embroiled in heated political debates to determine who would be the next leader of the free world. Meanwhile, Kaepernick's protest had become a global controversy concerning social injustices plaguing Black and brown people.

During a CNN town hall discussion, President Obama was asked whether he agreed with Kaepernick's protest.[5] He explained that first and foremost, Kaepernick was using his constitutional right to protest. But he also cautioned Kaepernick to consider the military families and others who associate with them who may be offended by his gesture. He finally expressed that people should also consider the reasoning behind Kaepernick's protest as a way to address the concerns Black people have over police brutality and other issues.

As the 2016 U.S. presidential election was nearing, media polls were showing that Trump and Clinton were closer than expected. Trump's "Make America Great Again" campaign slogan was a polarizing mechanism used to galvanize constituents who were tired of dealing with the last remnants of the 2008 economic recession and the politicians who were blamed for sending American jobs overseas. Clinton's "Stronger Together" campaign slogan was a chance to show that together, all Americans can work to make the country a stronger, more equitable country. This was a move away from Trump's notions of stepping into the Oval Office and repairing the government by himself. Still, he was able to build a strong base of supporters who believed in his agenda.

As the debates continued, Trump would go on to denounce the Black Lives Matter movement. In his speeches, he explained that the movement used divisive rhetoric that frowns upon the hardworking men and women who serve in law enforcement and the military. He said that all lives matter and that the country would be better off if leaders of the movement would stop dividing the country with their incendiary rhetoric. Lastly, he accused the movement of instigating a rise of violence against police officers and promised his supporters that he would launch an investigation into the organization if he became president.

For Republicans and other nonpartisan voters who believed in Trump's campaign, he was considered a refreshing take on perceived antiquated political promises of economic prosperity and job growth among the middle class. Additionally, his lack of following presidential protocol by sharing his various opinions via social media platforms showed voters that he was not going to be held back by political correctness.

Supporters of the Black Lives Matter movement encouraged voters not to support Trump in his campaign because the very meaning of "Make America Great Again" was considered a connection to the prosperous era of the mid-twentieth century, which was a time when Black people were not considered equal. On the other hand, supporters of the movement were encouraged to vote for Clinton, as she seemed the most likely to engage in policy work that supported equal rights and opportunities for all. Despite their pleas, Trump was elected as the forty-fifth president of the United States. It was during this time that he waged a war against the NFL.

SONS OF BITCHES, BOYCOTTS, AND BLACKBALLING

Before the start of the 2017 NBA Finals, LeBron James had one goal in mind: to cement his legacy as arguably the greatest basketball player in NBA history. Instead, his focus shifted to commenting on issues all too common to Black people in America. In James's response to the vandalism of his home, he not only expressed his exasperation for being Black in America, but he also confessed that "racism will always be a part of the world, a part of America."[6] While James's thoughts on racism may seem disheartening to some, it is a thought that is all too familiar for those who are victims of it. In addition to James's home being vandalized, three prominent areas in Washington's National Mall were vandalized with hate crime symbols. The first crime to occur was on May 27 when a noose was found in a tree near the Hirshhorn Museum. Just four days later, a noose was found near an exhibit at the National Museum of African American History and Culture. On June 2, a piece of rope was found near a bench at the Martin Luther King Jr. Memorial. Whether these were isolated incidents or works of a serial vandal, the issue of racism had once again reared its ugly head.

Before the start of the 2017 NFL season, Colin Kaepernick was told that he would not be re-signed by the 49ers organization because he was not a good fit with the new head coach, Kyle Shanahan's, offensive scheme.[7] Both the organization and Kaepernick agreed to mutually part ways so that Kaepernick could attempt to find a new team that would fit his skill set as a dual-threat quarterback. While he was still considered a top talent within the NFL, no teams were willing to sign him.

Speculation grew among spectators of the NFL that Kaepernick's inability to find a team was due to his anthem protests. Within the organization, it was rumored that several owners agreed with detractors of BLM on the notion that his actions were distasteful and disrespectful to law enforcement, which encouraged them not to sign him. Consequently, many settled on the belief that Kaepernick was blackballed—where one is rejected under a veil of secrecy—from the league. Despite this, Kaepernick continued denouncing police brutality and social injustice in society through various speaking engagements and his social media platform. Likewise, former teammate Eric Reid and other athletes around the sports world continued to take a knee and engage in other gestures in protest.

The NFL and other sports organizations continued to urge players to stand for the national anthem, but they were reluctant to punish athletes who exercised their constitutional right regarding freedom of speech. This did not sit well with President Trump. As Twitter became the social media outlet of choice during his presidency, he weighed in on the protest controversy by saying that Kaepernick should have been suspended because "you cannot disrespect our country, our flag, our anthem—you cannot do that."[8]

In their retort, several athletes, including Eric Reid, explained that their actions were not divisive. Rather, they explained that taking a knee was meant to be respectful to the military while also calling out injustices that continue to plague Black and brown people. They went on to say that any other interpretation regarding the reasoning behind their protests was an attempt to defame and deter any chance of criminal justice or societal reform that they sought. This, however, would not stop President Trump from holding the NFL accountable. During a presidential rally in Alabama, Trump said that owners who continuously see players protest should "get that son of a bitch off the field," to which the crowd's response was to repeatedly chant "U-S-A." He went on to say that anyone who saw anthem protests on television or while they were attending games should boycott the NFL.

Trump's criticism of the NFL drew the ire of NFL commissioner Roger Goodell. In a statement issued the day after the Alabama rally, Goodell said,

The NFL and our players are at our best when we help create a sense of unity in our country and culture. Divisive comments like these demonstrate an unfortunate lack of respect for the NFL, our great game, and all of the players, and a failure to understand the overwhelming force for good our clubs and players represent in our communities.[9]

As the 2017 NFL season continued, several reports began to display a decline in ratings.

A *Forbes* article blamed the decline on the oversaturation of the sport along with the changing viewing habits of consumers. More specifically, the article explained how the NFL's move to sign with online retail and streaming giant Amazon for their Thursday-night matchups created game fatigue among consumers who were already used to Sunday and Monday game schedules. In an ABC News article, it was reported that ratings went from 16.5 million viewers in 2016 to 14.9 million viewers in 2017.[10] The article also blamed the oversaturation of games through several networks and the national anthem controversy as the primary reasons for the decline in viewership. A *Sports Illustrated* article explained that several factors influenced the decline in viewership, including several popular franchises such as the New York Giants and the Dallas Cowboys having losing seasons.[11] However, President Trump blamed the decline of viewership on the notion that the games had become too boring and that viewers were tired of seeing the disrespect to the American flag.

TRUMP VERSUS THE NFL

In 2017, Colin Kaepernick, who had not played in the NFL since the end of the 2016 season, still was unsigned by any NFL team. While he remained in waiting, several NFL players continued their anthem protests against social injustice. This caused Trump to continue his attack against the NFL. He continuously sent out tweets admonishing the NFL for not taking action on player protests. NFL players who supported Kaepernick's initial protests began to also call out NFL owners for purposefully keeping him from being signed by teams. Supporters of Kaepernick who were outside the NFL were also critical of the NFL's continued denial of a contract.

Controversy continued to loom as then–vice president Mike Pence attended a regular-season game featuring the Indianapolis Colts and the San Francisco 49ers. As the former governor of Indiana, Pence said that he decided to attend the game in honor of the Colts' retiring former quarterback Peyton Manning's jersey number. At the playing of the national anthem, some 49er players knelt. Consequently, Pence left the game in opposition to the players protesting. In a subsequent tweet, Pence further explained his reasons for exiting:

I left today's Colts game because President Trump and I will not dignify any event that disrespects our soldiers, our Flag, or our National Anthem. At a time when so many Americans are inspiring our nation with their courage, resolve, and resilience, now, more than ever, we should rally around our Flag and everything that unites us. While everyone is entitled to their own opinions, I don't think it's too much to ask NFL players to respect the Flag and our National Anthem. I stand with President Trump, I stand with our soldiers, and I will always stand for our Flag and our National Anthem.[12]

Trump praised Pence as a leader who takes pride in being an American.

Eric Reid, who was one of a few 49ers players who protested during the game, felt that Pence's abrupt exit during the game was a public relations ploy geared toward causing a distraction from the true message behind the protests. He explained that these actions were the very reason why players began to protest in the first place. Kaepernick shared these sentiments as he formally filed a collusion grievance against the league. He retained attorney Mark Geragos, who had previously represented several high-profile individuals, to handle his negotiations moving forward. In his claim, Kaepernick expressed that he wanted an arbitration hearing due to the notion that the NFL and its owners have conspired to purposefully deny him employment in retaliation for his protest against racial and social injustice throughout the United States and globally. To further the point, Geragos reiterated,

If the NFL (as well as all professional sports teams) is to remain a meritocracy, then principled and peaceful protest—which the owners themselves made great theater imitating weeks ago—should not be punished and athletes should not be denied employment based on partisan political provocation by the Executive Branch of our government. Such a precedent threatens all patriotic Americans and harkens back to our darkest days as a nation. Protecting all athletes from such collusive conduct is what compelled Mr. Kaepernick to file his grievance.[13]

While Kaepernick did not directly file his grievance with the NFL Players Association (NFLPA), they released a statement showing their support for him as well as all players within the league.

WE HAVE HAD ENOUGH!

Many members of the NFL released several neutral statements neither condemning player protests nor lambasting the symbolism of the national anthem. But once Vice President Pence abruptly left the Colts and 49ers game, Dallas

Cowboys owner Jerry Jones decided to speak his mind. He said that he could no longer stand by and give the implication that his team or the NFL should continue to tolerate disrespecting the flag. He further threatened players by saying that if any player protested, he would forfeit the game.

This statement prompted owners and players to hold an emergency meeting to explore implementing an anthem policy that would require players to stand for the national anthem. Reports from the meeting drew the ire of many players as then-owner of the Houston Texans, Bob McNair, was heard saying that "the inmates should not be running the jailhouse." The comment reportedly started a heated discussion between players and owners. It became so heated that McNair issued a series of tweets via the Texans' public relations page apologizing to the public for his words. He then released the following tweet the next day to members of his organization where he explained what he meant by his statement:

> As I said yesterday, I was not referring to our players when I made a very re-gretful comment during the owner's meeting last week. I was referring to their relationship between the league office and team owners and how they have been making significant strategic decisions affecting our league without adequate input from ownership over the past few years. I am truly sorry to the players for how this has impacted them and the perception that it has created of me which could not be further from the truth. Our focus going forward, personally and as an organization, will be towards making meaningful progress regarding the social issues that mean so much to our players and our community.[14]

In the end, a vote did not take place. Rather, Commissioner Goodell held strong to the notion that NFL personnel should stand during the national anthem, as it is an important component of the game. Still, he did not establish a formal punishment for players who protested. Consequently, players throughout the league continued to protest for the remainder of the 2017 season.

The summer before the 2018 NFL season began with Kaepernick once again remaining unsigned by teams despite several NFL players believing that he was talented enough to have a roster spot. Athletes from several sports across the globe continued to engage in variations of protests regarding racial and social justice. Rating reports continued to show a decline in NFL viewership, in part due to the continued protests. However, reports were also showing that those who supported Kaepernick and the anthem protests had decided to stop watching the game until he was reinstated as a player. The league decided that reexamining a ban on anthem protests would be the best way to move forward.

Due to increased pressure, the NFL decided to enact a national anthem policy that required all league players and personnel who remained on the sideline to stand for the national anthem, with the option to stay in their respective locker rooms if they refused to stand.[15] Specifically, the NFL developed six guidelines that would describe the rules and penalties to athletes and teams should they choose not to stand during the playing of the national anthem:

1. All team and league personnel on the field shall stand and show respect for the flag and the anthem.
2. The Game Operations Manual will be revised to remove the requirement that all players be on the field for the anthem.
3. Personnel who choose not to stand for the anthem may stay in the locker room or a similar location off the field until after the anthem has been performed.
4. A club will be fined by the League if its personnel are on the field and do not stand and show respect for the flag and the anthem.
5. Each club may develop its own work rules, consistent with the above principles, regarding its personnel who do not stand and show respect for the flag and the anthem.
6. The commissioner will impose appropriate discipline on league personnel who do not stand and show respect for the flag and the anthem.[16]

This policy was approved by all team owners except for 49ers owner Jed York. His reasoning behind not supporting the policy was that he believed that players were not involved in the decision-making process.

In seeing the reports on the anthem policy, President Trump praised the league for taking a stance against what he claimed were unpatriotic players. While he was not happy about players having the option to sit in the locker room during the anthem, he said that this was a step in the right direction for patriotism. He would double down on the notion that players should be punished if they disrespected the flag by also mentioning that any player who continues to protest should no longer be in the NFL, let alone the country.

The NFLPA heavily critiqued the NFL for not collaborating with players in a resolution. Consequently, they filed a grievance against the league. It went as follows:

> Our union filed its non-injury grievance today on behalf of all players challenging the NFL's recently imposed anthem policy. The union claims that this new policy, imposed by the NFL's governing body without consultation with the NFLPA, is inconsistent with the collective bargaining agreement and infringes on player rights. In advance of our filing today, we proposed to the NFL to begin confidential discussions with the NFLPA Executive Committee to find a solution to this issue

instead of immediately proceeding with litigation. The NFL has agreed to proceed with those discussions and we look forward to starting them soon.[17]

The NFLPA further explained that the players were showing high levels of patriotism through their protests, activism, community service, and support for the military and their families. They finished by saying that not allowing them to engage in the anthem protest violated their constitutional rights. As a result, the NFL recanted their ruling until officials from both sides decided on the best approach to the anthem protests. This was much to the chagrin of President Trump.

BOYCOTT THE OVAL OFFICE

By now, tensions between athlete activists and President Trump had reached a breaking point. Many athletes from across many sports were tired of constantly explaining that the reasons behind their protest had nothing to do with the military. However, Trump and his constituents vehemently opposed the acts and considered them a detriment to the country. With the NFL rescinding their anthem protest policy, Trump decided to make a statement.

For years, professional and collegiate athletes had a tradition of visiting the White House upon winning championships associated with their particular sport. Likewise, it is traditional that U.S. presidents would invite those teams to participate in a ceremony with the president. But as criticism mounted against Trump for his denunciation of the Black Lives Matter movement and athlete activism, these traditions found themselves in jeopardy.

In the first two years of Trump's administration, twenty professional and collegiate teams who won championships were invited to the White House. However, only ten of these teams accepted the invitation. Of the teams that did not accept the invite, several players went on to express that Trump's chastisement of athletes engaging in activism was a clear sign that he and his followers were oblivious to the issues that Black and brown people face daily. One of the more vocal leaders in the movement to boycott an invitation to the White House was Golden State Warrior point guard Stephen Curry.

Following their 2017 NBA championship victory, Curry told reporters that he did not want to go to the White House. President Trump responded by saying that any NBA player who did not want to celebrate in the tradition of the White House visit should not bother showing up. After the team held a meeting on whether to attend, they decided that the best action was to not attend. Curry stated,

By acting and not going, hopefully that will inspire some change when it comes to what we tolerate in this country and what is accepted, and what we turn a blind eye to. It is not just the act of not going. There are things you have to do on the back end to push the message into motion.[18]

Instead, the team decided to visit the National Museum for African American History and Culture in the nation's capital.

In 2018, the Philadelphia Eagles were also disinvited by President Trump due to their support of athlete protests. Both Trump and team members expressed regret for the circumstance because the invite was also going to include events where children from the community would get chances to meet NFL stars. Still, many of the players on the team felt the necessity not to go due to Trump's disagreement with their activism. This move prompted another NFLPA statement in support of their players:

Our union is disappointed in the decision by the White House to disinvite players from the Philadelphia Eagles from being recognized and celebrated by all Americans for their accomplishments. This decision by the White House has led to the cancellation of several player-led community service events for young people in the Washington, DC area. NFL players love their country, support our troops, give back to their communities and strive to make America a better place.[19]

The Seattle Storm, who won the 2018 WNBA championship, was not invited to the White House and expressed that they would not attend even if they were. Storm player Sue Bird shared her initial excitement about the thought of visiting the White House but said that since Trump had been in office, the excitement has dissipated. Teammate Kaleena Mosqueda-Lewis supported Bird and added that if societal change did not occur, then it would become a commonplace occurrence for athletes not to attend the visit.

While these actions persisted, several high-profile athletes such as LeBron James took to social media to chastise Trump for not supporting athletes in their fight against social injustice. In an interview with then–ESPN reporter Cari Champion, James lamented his trials of being both a Black man and a high-profile athlete. Specifically, he discussed how he had to deal with someone vandalizing his home in 2017 by spray-painting the N-word on the gate leading to his property and how Trump's words regarding racial tensions in the United States were scary.

James's interview prompted Fox News host Laura Ingraham to criticize his thoughts. In her retort, she stated, "It's always unwise to seek political advice from someone who gets paid $100 million a year to bounce a ball. Keep the political comments to yourselves. . . . Shut up and dribble."[20] Ingraham's comments made national headlines as athletes accused her of egging on Trump's vitriol. James would respond by saying that "we will not shut up and dribble. . . . I mean too much to society, too much to the youth, too much to so many kids who feel like they don't have a way out." Little did James know that these sentiments would serve as one of the catalysts for athletes across various sports who were fighting for true social change.

CASE CLOSED

The start of the 2019 NFL season represented the third straight year that Colin Kaepernick remained unemployed. Eric Reid, who also filed a collusion grievance with the NFL, was let go from the 49ers, organization and was seeking employment. Before the 2019 season, however, Kaepernick and Reid attained a small victory in their grievance case when the NFL decided to settle with the players for an undisclosed amount of money.

As part of the settlement, both Kaepernick and Reid had to sign confidentiality agreements that required them to remain quiet regarding the terms of the agreement. However, details regarding the process of the grievance revealed that both players would face an uphill battle in showing the burden of proof for collusion as described in the NFLPA's collective bargaining agreement. As the rule mentioned,

> The failure by a club or clubs to negotiate, to submit offer sheets, or to sign contracts with restricted free agents or transition players, or to negotiate, make offers, or sign contracts for the playing services of such players or unrestricted free agents, shall not, by itself or in combination only with evidence about the playing skills of the player(s) not receiving any such offer or contract, satisfy the burden of proof set forth.[21]

In other words, Kaepernick and Reid could not claim collusion based on not being hired to play alone. Rather, they would also have to prove that owners, coaches, general managers, and other team personnel across the league agreed to purposefully deny employment. Nonetheless, both sides reached an agreement with a reported compensation of less than $10 million.

After news of the settlement broke, several notable figures reacted to the controversy. Former NBA player and current Hall of Famer Kareem Abdul-Jabbar praised the results of the grievance but expressed his frustrations with the fact that Kaepernick was still not signed by a team. Former ESPN news journalist and staunch supporter of Kaepernick, Jemele Hill, remained skeptical regarding the specificities of the settlement but challenged critics of Kaepernick by reinforcing that his talents were worthy of a roster spot on an NFL team. Former NFL running back Larry Johnson expressed that he wished

Kaepernick and Reid had not settled. Rather, he wanted them to take the league to trial as a challenge for them to become serious about social justice causes. Still, the settlement represented a modicum of success in determining how leaders within sports organizations were complicit in instances that were detrimental to marginalized people and, in particular, the issues that the Black Lives Matter movement was working to address.

WE SHALL OVERCOME

The rest of 2019 was full of trial and error, ebbing and flowing that constituted the relentless efforts of athletes fighting a perceivably endless fight against racial and social injustices. At the same time, the U.S. House of Representatives filed two articles of impeachment against President Trump. The first article focused on the belief that Trump abused his power while in office. The second article focused on obstruction of Congress. Collectively, the charge against him was that he allegedly used his power to coerce Ukrainian president Volodymyr Zelensky to investigate the Democratic Party as a way to influence his reelection.

Despite the formal impeachment articles, approval ratings for Trump remained high. According to an article by Morning Consult, he received a record number of approval votes by members of the Republican Party.[22] Much of his job performance ratings came from his campaign promises of increased jobs and decreased taxes. Additionally, he was also praised by members of the Republican Party because of his ardent stance against athletes and sports leagues whom he considered unpatriotic and disrespectful when it came to supporting military members and loving the country.

Despite the back-and-forth debate, the NFL relented and offered Colin Kaepernick a private workout where all thirty-two teams were invited to attend. However, negotiations regarding the terms of the workout quickly fell apart as Kaepernick believed that the league was not fully transparent in how the workout would shape out. Therefore, he decided to change the venue from the Atlanta Falcons workout facilities to a local Atlanta-area high school. Several factors influenced his decision. First, he wanted to sign a traditional NFL injury waiver. But the NFL wanted to amend the waiver that ensured nonguarantees of employment clauses. Second, Kaepernick was concerned that he would not have a copy of workout recordings and requested that he have his production crew on site. The NFL also denied this request. Third, in an attempt to reach common ground regarding the recording of his workouts, Kaepernick requested that they allow local and national media to attend his workout session. The NFL still would not honor the request. After the NFL failed to compromise with Kaepernick, he decided to invite NFL personnel to another venue that would not only showcase his talents but help him control the narrative.

While reports from the workout showed that Kaepernick still had NFL-caliber skills even after three years of not being signed to a roster, the workout resulted in no signing. Mixed reviews followed as some individuals said that the NFL was engaging in a publicity stunt to show that they gave Kaepernick an opportunity. Others blamed both sides because no signed documentation held either party liable.

The mounting vitriol regarding the unfair treatment Kaepernick was receiving from the NFL, Trump's continued fight against athletes and the overall Black Lives Matter movement, and the larger political unrest regarding social injustice were putting a strain on global race relations. However, no one expected that a global pandemic would help spark a more succinct and structured movement where athletes would use their platforms to move from protest to policy reform.

Chapter Four

We Want Reform

While several athletes joined in the national anthem protests in 2016, Colin Kaepernick stood out as the most influential. His protests stirred conversations from the high school bleachers to the Oval Office. As of the writing of this chapter, he still has not been signed by an NFL team. However, this did not stop him from pursuing avenues to engage in tangible social justice.

There were several similarities between the anthem protest and Muhammad Ali's refusal to go to war during the civil rights era. Both movements demonstrated a double standard by the American government, which praised a country that was fair and free to all while Black people faced a harsh reality of discriminatory acts. Whereas civil rights–era athletes were seemingly powerless in challenging sports organizations to be better for society, today's athletes have accepted the challenge to engage in reform that benefits all marginalized individuals.

As mentioned in chapter 2, the Black Lives Matter (BLM) movement created an international conversation on racial justice and police reform. Consequently, Black athletes began demonstrating their disdain for social injustices. But it was the anthem protests that began the rise of sport as a platform for social justice advocacy that challenged local, state, and federal legislation. Therefore, we began to see the transition away from athlete activists as protesters. We now see them as social justice reformers.

During the 2016 NFL season in which he protested, Kaepernick decided to take things a step further by establishing a nonprofit organization geared toward fighting oppression. Aptly named Know Your Rights Camps, Kaepernick wanted to raise awareness among youth of what to do if they were to ever encounter police. Additionally, he pledged $1 million of his salary to fund nonprofit organizations that shared his mission.

Regarding the Know Your Rights Camp, he developed a ten-point system motivating youth and young adults to understand their rights to be productive, responsible citizens in this country. These points are as follows:

> You have the right to be free. You have the right to be healthy. You have the right to be brilliant. You have the right to be safe. You have the right to be loved. You have the right to be courageous. You have the right to be alive. You have the right to be trusted. You have the right to be educated. You have the right to know your rights.[1]

To this day, he continues to run the organization, which now educates youth and young adults from around the country.

In 2017, NFL athletes became outraged at team owners and the commissioner for not caring about issues that plagued the Black community. In response to this and the perceived blackballing of Kaepernick from the game, players decided to form the Players Coalition to improve social justice and racial equality in the United States. Spearheaded by former NFL players Anquan Boldin and Malcolm Jenkins, the Players Coalition gained section 501(c)(4) recognition under the Internal Revenue Code to "achieve social justice and racial equality by pressing lawmakers to support effective policies and programs to end systemic inequality and racism through criminal justice reform."[2]

The Players Coalition challenges the NFL to become committed to eradicating social injustice and led to a mutual partnership in which the league committed $90 million to causes that are important to the Black community. In the deal, the NFL designated the funds over seven years for local and national projects to make communities better. The Players Coalition may have appreciated the partnership with the NFL, but the league also had a further agenda.

The league's hope with the partnership was both to reiterate that players should stand during the national anthem and to influence players not to engage in protests.[3] But the coalition and other athletes from across the country insisted that if the NFL was to pledge against social injustice while Colin Kaepernick was still not being signed by a team, then their words were null and void.

In 2018, Nike became one of the first major corporate organizations to support Kaepernick's initial protest for social justice by developing an ad campaign that featured him. Titled "Dream Crazy," it featured Kaepernick speaking on following one's dream. The most popular slogan from the ad was "Believe in something. Even if it means sacrificing everything."[4] Despite the vitriol from some Americans, the ad became very popular, so much so that

Kaepernick's 49ers jersey sales became the most popular-selling jersey, even though he still was without an NFL contract.

The move by Nike to support Kaepernick was instrumental in the fight against social injustice as athletes were beginning to understand that they had to initiate change in both the public and the private sectors. Between 2016 and 2019, NFL athletes continued to make strides in change. However, 2020 would be the year that athletes from other sports began making strides in pushing for policy reform.

THE YEAR THAT WASN'T

On November 17, 2019, reports were emanating regarding a virus out of Hubei Province in China. Initially going unrecognized, more reports developed as several other cases of the virus began to surface. By January 2020, the World Health Organization (WHO) reported on a novel virus that was first located in Wuhan, China, that first presented pneumonia-like symptoms. At that time, almost sixty cases of the virus were presented globally, including the first case in the United States. This prompted the WHO to declare a global health emergency. In February, President Trump declared a U.S. public health emergency for the now-named COVID-19 virus. At this time there were over nine thousand global cases and two hundred deaths reported. By March, the WHO declared COVID-19 a global pandemic. The effects of the pandemic sent the world into a shutdown period in which individuals were encouraged to only make trips outside of their homes when necessary. This wreaked havoc on the sports world.

On March 11, 2020, the National Basketball Association announced via their Twitter account that the rest of the NBA season would be suspended until further notice. The following day, the 2020 NCAA Division I men's and women's basketball tournament, colloquially called "March Madness," was canceled. This was the first time that the men's and women's tournaments were canceled since their inception in 1939 and 1982, respectively. As the sports world was reeling in the midst of the pandemic, police brutality issues continued to plague the Black community. Two of the more notable incidents were those involving Kentucky resident Breonna Taylor and Minnesota resident George Floyd.

On March 13, 2020, Taylor was shot and killed by Louisville police officers who were responding to a drug deal investigation in the apartments she was living in. Her boyfriend, Kenneth Walker, was also an occupant in the apartment at the time of her death. As the reports described, Taylor and Walker were in their home as plainclothes officers first knocked, announced themselves, and then forced entry into their home. Walker, who said that he did not hear an announcement, fired a warning shot to scare potential intruders. Upon hearing the shot, the officers responded by firing thirty-two shots into the apartment. Six of the bullets hit Taylor, subsequently killing her.

On May 25, 2020, forty-six-year-old George Floyd was stopped by Minneapolis police officers after a store clerk suspected him of using counterfeit money as payment. While being arrested, Floyd was placed on the ground where police officer Derek Chauvin began kneeling on his neck and back. Chauvin stayed in this position for nine minutes and twenty-nine seconds, which ultimately resulted in Floyd's death.

Weeks of protest ensued after Taylor's and Floyd's deaths. Multiple reports showed that the nation engaged in the largest racial protest in the United States since the civil rights movement. The Black Lives Matter movement led these protests and also catalyzed a global movement against social injustice. For example, over twenty thousand protesters took to the streets in London to call out systemic racism across the UK. In New Zealand, Black protesters were galvanized after the George Floyd murder to speak out about racial injustices that they believe government officials have largely ignored. In France, protesters called out government officials over what they felt were systemic issues that still held on to antiquated colonialist tactics that ensured violence against their Black citizens. In Colombia, citizens were galvanized by both Floyd's death and the death of others by the police force.[5] In one of the deadlier incidents following Floyd's death, Columbia citizens expressed that they were no longer afraid of death at the hands of the police in a challenge against police brutality that continuously plagues the country. Still, it was the outcry within the United States that caused a more focused movement by athletes globally.

THE AWAKENING

According to the *Washington Post*, the murder of George Floyd prompted the largest protest movement in U.S. history. More so, "an estimated 15 million to 26 million people participated in protests in all 50 states and on every continent except Antarctica amid the global covid-19 pandemic."[6] Floyd's death would also awaken the sports world to a push for societal change that hasn't been seen since the civil rights movement.

National Association for Stock Car Auto Racing (NASCAR) driver Bubba Wallace spoke out on racial injustice and police brutality against Black people at the hands of the police. Wallace, who is African American, subsequently became the unofficial spokesperson for BLM within NASCAR.

Next, Wallace challenged NASCAR to remove the Confederate flag from their events. The organization obliged by discontinuing the use of the flag at their games and by requesting that fans no longer display the flag at events. While some fans abided by the rules, others continued to showcase the flag. This led NASCAR officials to permanently ban the flag from being displayed at their events. This encouraged Wallace to continue his support for the BLM movement.

During the Blue-Emu Maximum Pain Relief 500 race, Wallace applied a custom paint scheme to his car that displayed "#BlackLivesMatter" on the side while also showing a pair of Black and white hands interlocking. The final scheme on the car showcased the words "Compassion, Love, and Understanding." This message was inspired by Wallace's wish for a world where all lives could live and prosper equally. Wallace later made national headlines when a member of the team reported that a noose was placed in his garage stall at Talladega Superspeedway. The incident, which took place before the Geico 500 race, prompted NASCAR officials to denounce the act and seek assistance from law enforcement. Wallace also expressed that he was deeply saddened by the matter and that America has a long way to go for racial reconciliation. During the race, other drivers showed solidarity by pushing Wallace's car to the front of the pit road.

After the race, the FBI launched an investigation into the incident. They discovered that the noose was not in direct relation to Wallace and his ethnicity. Instead, they said that the rope was a pull-down rope tied in the style of a hangman's knot. Upon receiving news of the report, detractors began blaming Wallace for inciting division and creating false reports. One of the more vocal critics of Wallace was President Trump. In a series of tweets, Trump further denounced the Black Lives Matter movement by branding the incident as a hoax. He criticized NASCAR officials by saying that they should not have banished the display of the Confederate flag at their events. He then said that NASCAR ratings are low because of the Confederate flag removal. Fox Sports, which broadcasts NASCAR events, denied the claims made by Trump.

With the FBI's findings regarding the noose, Wallace said that he was glad the incident was not targeted at him. But he was angered by the backlash he received claiming that he had made up the entire scenario to spark controversy. Several prominent athletes continued to show their support for Wallace despite the backlash. Additionally, NASCAR president Steve Phelps went on to implement implicit bias training that would serve as the organization's wave of action to eradicate prejudice and discrimination within the sport.

WE'LL TAKE IT FROM HERE!

In addition to instances of police brutality, the summer of 2020 saw a nation reeling from the coronavirus pandemic. Still, sports teams were trying to discover the best ways to salvage their seasons. NBA commissioner Adam Silver and his staff agreed upon a shortened regular season and play-off scenario that would take place in one sectioned-off arena. Dubbed the "NBA bubble," players would continue to play their games without an audience and away from close acquaintances located at Walt Disney World in Bay Lake, Florida. Similarly, the WNBA would create their bubble at the IMG Academy (IMG) in Bradenton, Florida. More so, it would be the WNBA that would set the tone for activism in 2020.

While many Black people and allies were waiting on justice for the Breonna Taylor shooting, the WNBA decided to take action. When the league resumed playing within their bubble at IMG, they decided to dedicate their season to seeking justice for Breonna Taylor. As mentioned, Taylor was killed by Louisville, Kentucky, police officers earlier that year during a botched search altercation. As part of their dedication, WNBA players established a social justice council that convened to discuss ways in which policy reform on racism, sexism, and other societal injustices could be established. To further establish momentum, players donned BLM T-shirts promoting "Say Her Name" as a means to garner attention for police brutality issues against women.

Alicia Garza, who is one of the founding members of BLM, served as one of the many notable advisors to the social justice council. The Women's National Basketball Players Association (WNBPA) president, Nneka Ogwumike, reinforced the collective commitment that players would make to ensure that justice would happen. She said,

> As many WNBA players—past and present—have said and, more importantly, consistently demonstrated, the reason why you see us engaging and leading the charge when it comes to social advocacy is that it is in our DNA. With 140-plus voices all together for the first time, we can be a powerful force connecting to our sisters across the country and in other parts of the world. And may we all recognize that the league's stated commitment to us—in this season and beyond—offers a pivotal moment in sports history.[7]

As social justice efforts continued, the WNBA became known as one of the first sports leagues that established a collective effort for social justice. Throughout the history of activism, individuals were typically at the forefront of the movement. But the WNBA's collective efforts set a tone that would start a chain reaction for other sports leagues to use their collective powers to establish policy reform.

NO MORE TALK!

As the country was still working through the pandemic, sports leagues began to take action on establishing larger platforms for their athletes to speak to social justice issues. The NFL, which had been highly criticized for their treatment of Colin Kaepernick, admitted to their inadequacies in how they handled social justice issues. In a statement by the league commissioner, Roger Goodell, he explained how the league could do better in supporting Black people. Specifically, he said,

> We, the National Football League, admit we were wrong for not listening to NFL players earlier and encourage all to speak out and peacefully protest. We, the National Football League, believe Black lives matter.[8]

To showcase that they were committed to supporting Black people, the NFL announced a ten-year deal that would donate $250 million to several organizations that combat systemic racism in the United States. Still, police brutality persisted.

On August 23, 2020, another Black man was shot by police officers. Then–twenty-nine-year-old Wisconsin resident Jacob Blake was involved in an alleged domestic dispute when 9-1-1 dispatchers were called to the scene. Blake, who had previous warrants regarding sexual assault, was reportedly trying to break up an altercation with two women. One of the women was Blake's girlfriend. Witnesses reported that Blake reached for a knife to help end the altercation between the two women.

Once the police arrived, Blake walked back to his girlfriend's car. Witnesses said that a small child was sitting in the backseat of the car. Police reports indicated that Blake wielded the knife toward them. Consequently, to ensure the safety of the child and that of the two women involved in the dispute, they felt compelled to stop him by any means necessary. Therefore, the officers shot Blake while he was leaning into the vehicle. He did not succumb to the wounds, but they left him partially paralyzed.

National protests ensued as legal experts, BLM supporters, and allies called for the federal government to investigate the matter and punish the officers involved in the incident. In one of the deadlier protests in recent years, two civilians were gunned down and one was wounded by a white, armed civilian named Kyle Rittenhouse. Rittenhouse, who was seventeen years old at the time, would serve as a platform for BLM supporters to illuminate the perceivable double standard America has when it comes to shooting incidents in which the perpetrator is white versus when the perpetrator is Black.

Upon hearing of Blake's shooting, teams within the NBA bubble took action. The Milwaukee Bucks convened before their play-off game and decided to boycott their game. In their reasoning behind the boycotts, the players felt that playing basketball did not matter when larger societal wrongs regarding racial injustice and police brutality continued to happen. Additionally, the players declared that unless the NBA engaged in a collaborative effort to end injustice, they would continue to protest.

After heated discussions between players, coaches, and league front office members, the NBA decided to postpone the other play-off games scheduled for that day. This caused a chain reaction as the WNBA, MLB, and MLS postponed their games for the day to show solidarity with Blake and the BLM movement. Tennis superstar Naomi Osaka also joined the protest by declaring that she would not play in the Western and Southern Open semifinals.

As a resolution, the NBA and NBPA negotiated a deal where the league and team owners would establish a formal platform that would work to create better socioeconomic standards in the Black community. Consequently, the NBA Board of Governors contributed $300 million to establish the NBA Foundation. This foundation represented one of the first moves by any sports organization to concentrate on economic empowerment that would allow members of the Black community to engage in positive generational empowerment. Additionally, the foundation is guided by three pillars: helping members of the Black community obtain a first job, assistance in securing employment beyond high school or college, and avenues for upward mobility while employed.

In a statement released by NBPA executive director Michele Roberts, she stated,

> Given the resources and incredible platform of the NBA, we have the power to ideate, implement, and support substantive policies that reflect the core principles of equality and justice we embrace. This foundation will provide a framework for us to stay committed and accountable to these principles.[9]

In a similar statement, NBA commissioner Adam Silver said,

> We are dedicated to using the collective resources of the 30 teams, the players, and the league to drive meaningful economic opportunities for Black Americans. We believe that through focused programs in our team markets and nationally, together with clear and specific performance measures, we can advance our shared goals of creating substantial economic mobility within the Black community.[10]

One of the first calls to action from these newly formed professional sports initiatives was to push Congress to eradicate police brutality. Collectively, over 1,100 athletes and coaches and over 300 front office personnel across the NFL, MLB, and NBA charged Congress to pass the Ending Qualified

Immunity Act. The goal of this act was to ensure that law enforcement would be held liable for misconduct in the field. This would not be the only push by athletes toward local, state, and federal governments.

GO VOTE!

With the pandemic and police brutality making tensions flare throughout the United States, 2020 also represented an election year. Supporters of Trump praised his "Make America Great Again" mantra, while denouncers expressed that his four-year term was full of divisiveness that showed a lack of concern for marginalized people. Consequently, a push was made by athletes and other high-profile individuals to encourage registered voters to vote for officials who would work to establish an equitable society for all people. However, a focal concern for these individuals was the long-standing history of voter suppression among minority voters.

In a *USA Today* article, former Los Angeles Clipper head coach Doc Rivers explained how his father was instrumental in establishing equal voting rights for Black people during the civil rights era.[11] His father, who was a cop in a Chicago suburb, said that poll workers would force Black voters to submit to a literacy test before turning in their ballot. Such practices were common during that time. But many people have suggested that similar barriers exist to this day. Consequently, athletes began using their platform to call out other organizations to end these discriminatory practices.

In the months before Election Day, voting fraud and equal voting rights became the talk of the nation. Many individuals from marginalized communities wanted to vote but felt disenfranchised by polling centers and other voting outlets. To help close this gap, several lawmakers urged the federal government to increase funding to support the United States Postal Service (USPS) in their mail-in balloting efforts. President Trump and his supporters discouraged this request because they believed that increased funding would encourage voter fraud. An outcry ensued as members of the Democratic Party and society at large felt that the president's denial of funding to the USPS was a way of guaranteeing his victory for a second term. The national outcry continued as many individuals feared that President Trump would earn a second term.

In response to voter inequity, the NBA and NBPA developed campaigns to create awareness for better civic engagement and voter awareness. Throughout the 2020 season, over twenty-three teams opened their arenas to engage in various voter registration activities. Additionally, the league and the players' association partnered with nonprofit organizations, players, and nonpartisan political organizations to spread the word regarding the importance of voting. Some of their partners included organizations such as When We All Vote, a national organization seeking to demystify the process of voting and ensure the closure of discriminatory gaps related to voting. Also, the NBA was instrumental in supporting national voter movements including National Voter Registration Day, National Black Voter Day, and National Vote Early Day, among others. Further, the NBA partnered with Black Entertainment Television (BET), the National Urban League (NUL), the NAACP, and other civic organizations to push for equality at the voting polls.

The WNBA also used its platform to raise awareness of voter suppression through several campaigns. One of the more profound movements was the "Unite the Vote" challenge that was constructed by nine of the twelve WNBA teams. Through this challenge, the teams developed individualized campaigns for their fan base through friendly competitions as a way to increase voter participation. The competition, which lasted from August 18 to September 18, 2020, represented the one hundredth anniversary of the Nineteenth Amendment, which extended the right to vote for white women but did not provide equal opportunity for Black women.[12] In a statement released by Washington Mystic senior vice president Alycen McAuley, she explained that the team organized with the other eight teams to highlight the importance of voting for all marginalized individuals, particularly among Black women, whom they deem are still overlooked when it comes to racial equality. Through their efforts, over 90 percent of WNBA players became registered voters. However, a pivotal moment in their campaign would prove vital to the movement.

As WNBA players gained national attention for their commitments to social justice, one team owner expressed her disdain. Atlanta Dream co-owner and Georgia senator Kelly Loeffler (R-GA) wrote a scathing letter to WNBA leadership criticizing their support of the BLM movement. Specifically, she wrote,

> I adamantly oppose the Black Lives Matter political movement, which has advocated for the defunding of police, called for the removal of Jesus from churches and the disruption of the nuclear family structure, harbored anti-Semitic views, and promoted violence and destruction across the country. I believe it is misaligned with the values of the WNBA and the Atlanta Dream, where we support tolerance and inclusion.[13]

This statement caused WNBA players to intensify their efforts for social change.

The league partnered with the NBA on several initiatives including Hoopers Vote, More Than a Vote, and other campaigns dedicated to equal voting opportunities. Also, they continued to show support to the BLM movement by wearing T-shirts and having a BLM logo displayed on the basketball court. More so, many players announced that they would show their support for Rev. Raphael Warnock, who was the main challenger to Senator Loeffler. Little did Loeffler know that her actions would compel one of her players to push for an ownership change.

Atlanta Dream guard Renee Montgomery sent out a tweet to Loeffler expressing her disappointment with the owner's sentiments regarding BLM. Specifically, she said,

> When Black Lives Matter started, the founders never thought that they would have to add the word "too" at the end of it: Black Lives Matter Too. We just assumed that people would understand that we matter also. Is that too big of an ask?[14]

To further push her mission for systemic change, Montgomery convened with a team of investors that sought to buy out Loefflers's stake with the Dream. This move was a success as Montgomery, who sat out during the 2020 season to work on social justice, became vice president and co-owner of the team in February 2021. Montgomery was not the only WNBA player to sit out the 2020 season to combat social injustice.

Minnesota Lynx forward Maya Moore, who took a sabbatical from the WNBA in 2019, expressed that she found a new calling of reforming the American justice system. During this time, she worked to exonerate Missouri native Jonathan Irons. Irons, who had been in prison for over two decades, was convicted of assault with a deadly weapon and armed robbery. With her diligence, she was able to convince a Missouri judge that prosecutors had withheld evidence that would have aided in Irons's case. Consequently, his conviction was vacated. Moore and Irons went on to get married and have committed to fully advocating for wrongfully convicted people of color.

Election Day proved vital to several social causes heading into 2021 as former vice president Joe Biden was elected as the forty-seventh president of the United States. President Trump blamed his loss on allegations of electoral fraud by states that counted mail-in ballots. His continued allegations of voter fraud caused his supporters to engage in one of the more heinous crimes against the U.S. Capitol in history. On January 6, 2021, supporters of President Trump engaged in an attack on the Capitol during a joint session of Congress for hearings on electoral voting. Overall, nearly 140 police officers were injured, and several individuals either died or were injured during the attack. Following the attack, President Trump conceded, and President Biden took over.

ONWARD AND UPWARD

As LeBron James and other high-profile athletes continued using their platform for social change, other athletes criticized those who involved themselves in political discourse. For example, soccer superstar Zlatan Ibrahimovic would express his views regarding LeBron speaking up about social injustice via UEFA for Discovery+:

> LeBron is phenomenal at what he's doing, but I don't like when people have some kind of status, they go and do politics at the same time. Do what you're good at. Do the category you do. I play football because I'm the best at playing football. I don't do politics. If I would be a political politician, I would do politics.[15]

In response to this comment, LeBron said,

> I would never shut up about things that's wrong. I preach about my people and I preach about equality, social injustice, racism, systematic voter suppression, things that go in our community. Because I was a part of my community at one point and seeing the things that was going on and I know what's going on still because I have a group of 300-plus kids at my school that's going through the same thing and they need a voice. And I'm their voice. I'm their voice and I use my platform to continue to shed light on everything that may be going on not only in my community but around this country and around the world.[16]

Despite this, athletes continued to fight for reform.

To control police brutality within the state of Maryland, members from the Washington Commanders football team testified before the Maryland House Judiciary Committee during a virtual hearing. The meeting, which was held on February 9, 2021, was led by Washington Commanders defensive end Chase Young and other teammates. They hoped to bring awareness to police reform by establishing a use-of-force policy for police officers who get into altercations with suspects. Specifically, the policy would ban police chokeholds and no-knock warrants and would require every police department within the state to have officers wear body cameras by 2025. If passed, House Bill 670 would be the official legislation, and it would repeal the Law Enforcement Bill of Rights. These included giving officers a formal waiting period before they had to cooperate with internal inquiries into police conduct, scrubbing records of complaints brought against officers after a certain period, and ensuring that only fellow officers—not civilians—could investigate them. If repealed, it would potentially set a nationwide precedent on police accountability.

While politics have been connected to sports for quite a while, what many may not know is that sports organizations often establish committees that donate to politicians that fit their ideologies. For example, the NFL established a political action committee, or PAC for short, entitled Gridiron. Through this PAC, the NFL has contributed millions to several politicians and lobbying efforts. Of concern to the concepts of bipartisanship, the NFL has been found to primarily donate to Republican candidates.

In a 2020 report by sports media website The Athletic, the PAC made sixty-three total donations to government leaders and political organizations.[17] Of the sixty-three, fifty-two were made to those with Republican interests. The NFL is not the only major sports organization to have its own PAC. Major League Baseball has operated its own PAC since 2002. Similar to the NFL, MLB has also spent millions in lobbying and donations to political parties, but not as much as the NFL. An argument can be made that sports leagues are only seeking to provide standards for their bottom-line agendas; however, the call for sports organizations to be more accountable toward social causes could make many speculate whose interests are more important depending on who these organizations donate to. This could become a problem when it comes to issues such as voter suppression.

In 2021, Georgia Republicans signed a ninety-eight-page document into law that curtails ballot access for voters in booming urban and suburban counties, home to many Democrats. Another provision makes it a crime to offer water to voters waiting in lines, which tend to be longer in densely populated communities. Black people who lived in Georgia identified other stipulations to the law that violated their voting rights.

First, with the new law, voters are no longer allowed to use signature matching to identify themselves when it comes to absentee balloting. Instead, voters would have to have proof of a valid Georgia driver's license number or state identification number. A CNN article on voting rights reported that approximately two hundred thousand state citizens lack the identification requirements for the new law.[18] Voting rights organizations including Rise Inc. and the Black Voters Matter Fund have criticized the law for making voting difficult for Black Georgians.

Second, an analysis regarding the length of time to vote collected by Georgia Public Broadcasting and ProPublica reported inequalities in terms of wait time for voting. Specifically, the report explained that after the 7 p.m. scheduled poll-closing time, nonwhites would have to wait almost an hour after polls closed, juxtaposed to just six minutes when it came to white voters.

As a result of the voting rights issue, MLB decided to remove the 2021 All-Star game from Georgia as a gesture of solidarity toward eradicating voter suppression. Fred Ridley, who serves as the Augusta National and Masters chairman, was indifferent about the matter. He would say,

> The right to vote is fundamental in our democratic society. No one should be disadvantaged in exercising that right, and it is critical that all citizens have confidence in the electoral process. This is fundamental to who we are as a people. We realize that views and opinions on this law differ, and there have been calls for boycotts and other punitive measures. Unfortunately, those actions often impose the greatest burdens on the most vulnerable in our society. And in this case, that includes our friends and neighbors here in Augusta who are the very focus of the positive difference we are trying to make.[19]

Athlete activism not only helped to lessen a long-standing problem with voting rights in the United States, but some athletes focused on the socioeconomic well-being of marginalized individuals as well. For example, NBA superstar Kyrie Irving developed a business consulting firm called KAI 11 Consulting LLC in 2021. With this firm, Irving seeks to provide consulting services that offer programs and mentoring to underrepresented business owners seeking assistance in cultivating and scaling their business.

The creation of this consulting firm was preceded by a leave of absence that Irving took to focus on personal matters during the 2021 NBA season. His time off included visiting Little Rock Central High School in Little Rock, Arkansas, to understand the history of segregation in education in the United States. Upon his return to the NBA, his focus shifted to Black empowerment while also holding those in power accountable for the January 2021 insurrection on the Capitol.

Even concerns regarding mental health and sport began to gain traction. For years, the NFL has been wrought with controversy over the issue of concussions within the sport. Particularly, the league has been under scrutiny for denying the impact of chronic traumatic encephalopathy, or CTE, on its players. First brought to the NFL's attention by forensic pathologist Dr. Bennett Omalu, CTE became an increasingly evident phenomenon within the sport.

As the issue of CTE gained national attention, doctors began to focus on how many athletes were negatively affected. Dr. Ann McKee, who serves as the CTE Center director at Boston University, recently reported that over three hundred former NFL players have been found to have the disease, with many of those who have died from the disease being between the ages of twenty and forty. As a result of this information, the NFL has agreed to a $1 billion settlement on brain injury claims from former players.

Additionally, the NFL had decided to stop the use of race norming against Black players. Under this concept, Black players were assumed to have lower baseline levels of cognitive functioning than white players. Black claimants, then, had to demonstrate more impairment to receive the same financial awards as their white counterparts.[20]

To date, more than two thousand former NFL players have filed lawsuits claiming dementia and other related cognitive issues, but more than half of them have yet to receive financial benefits. Still, the settlement revealed the glaring issues related to concussions while ultimately garnering the perception that the NFL has known of the link between concussions and long-term brain injury for some time.

WE STAND WITH YOU!

During the late '80s and early '90s, athlete activism was all but over. As mentioned in chapter 1, much of this lack of activism was due to exorbitant contracts and endorsement deals that athletes were afraid of losing. Additionally, athletes were discouraged by their teams and league officials from engaging in political stances at the risk of suspension or being blackballed. Affiliate sports organizations also discouraged these actions. Sport apparel organizations such as Nike and Adidas spent decades remaining apolitical. Additionally, global sport and entertainment firms such as Octagon and Anschutz Entertainment Group (AEG) followed suit in their hesitancy to engage in political stances. However, societal calls for racial justice have slowly shifted the bottom-line agenda of these brands.

The BLM movement paved the way for the revitalization of athlete activism. Nike became one of the first major brands to engage in athlete activism when they released a 2018 ad featuring Colin Kaepernick supporting his cause for eradicating police brutality and racial injustice. As high-profile police shootings permeated the media landscape, athlete activists continued to raise their voices under the banner of BLM. Their efforts not only showed sports leagues that they could no longer be silent on racial injustice, but the movement also challenged sport-affiliated brands to change as well.

In a 2020 Nielsen poll, 72 percent of sports fans believed that athletes should be involved in the BLM movement.[21] Additionally, 77 percent of sports fans believed that brands are more powerful when they partner with sports organizations to help influence social change. Considering this, it makes sense that several affiliated brands would speak out in support of sports organizations' involvement in the BLM movement during that year. On June 2, 2020, global sports brand Under Armour released a tweet supporting the BLM movement. Specifically, they said,

> Black Lives Matter. There's nothing we can say right now that is more important or powerful than the voices of our Black community. We stand for equality and

are dedicated to elevating the voices of our Black athletes and teammates. More to come.[22]

South Korean sportswear company Fila posted on their Instagram account that they decided to donate $100,000 U.S. dollars to the BLM organization. German sports apparel company Puma also posted on their Instagram their donation to the Minnesota Freedom Fund in the wake of the George Floyd killing. Additionally, they posted a picture of the 1968 Olympics protest, further suggesting that the world needs to take action on social injustice. American outwear and sportswear company Columbia Sportswear released several statements via their website supporting the BLM movement and individuals who stand up against racial injustice in the wake of the police killings involving Jacob Blake and George Floyd. To pay respects to Floyd's death, Columbia closed their North American stores for two hours during his memorial service.

As Nike remains the number one sportswear brand in the world based on revenue and arguably one of the most recognized overall brands, they continued their support of Kaepernick and athletes fighting for social justice globally. On June 5, 2020, they announced a four-year, $40 million commitment to the Black community via their joint Nike, Jordan, and Converse brands. A statement released by company CEO John Donahoe said,

> Systemic racism and the events that have unfolded across America over the past few weeks serve as an urgent reminder of the continued change needed in our society. We know Black Lives Matter. We must educate ourselves more deeply on the issues faced by Black communities and under the enormous suffering and senseless tragedy racial bigotry creates.[23]

Despite their efforts, many supporters of the BLM movement fear that brands are only showing their support to follow a trend instead of engaging in tangible and sustainable social justice reform. This makes sense considering the history of such brands remaining silent on controversial political stances. At the least, however, supporting athletes and BLM has removed the taboo status of racial justice from the intersection of sport and politics. Still, instances of social injustice continued.

DON'T CALL ME AN AMATEUR!

Similar to professional sports, the pandemic has caused the cancellation of several college sporting events. What is dissimilar is the amateur status that student-athletes have, which limits their maneuverability and stability.

Throughout the 2020 season, several regional collegiate athletic associations and NCAA tournaments were canceled as the pandemic continued to affect global health and safety. While all student-athletes have had to cope with the volatile ebbing and flowing of the pandemic, those from marginalized backgrounds are particularly vulnerable. What has helped is the new ruling regarding athlete compensation.

As professional athletes from across the nation were finding their voices in the fight against social injustice, college athletes began to recognize their power. For decades, student-athletes have lamented that they do not share a part of the NCAA's revenue. As mentioned in chapter 2, the NCAA generates most of its earnings from high-revenue-generating sports such as men's football and basketball. Through various championship series, bowl games, and basketball tournaments, the NCAA earns billions of dollars a year in sponsorships and advertisements. Considering that most of the players who participate in the sports are Black, several activists, parents, media outlets, and others have drawn comparisons of student-athlete treatment to slave labor given the immense level of sanctions the NCAA could levy if student-athletes were to receive any level of compensation. To understand these sanctions, one must examine the NCAA's history.

The NCAA was established in 1906 under the initial name Intercollegiate Athletic Association of the United States (IAAUS). It was formed as a regulatory association for college athletics as a way to provide reforms that worked to eliminate the injuries and deaths of athletes that were plaguing colleges. Initially run by university chancellors, the NCAA began to recognize that the continued growth and popularity of college athletics would prove too difficult to be run by a consortium of colleges. Consequently, they made a move that would establish the NCAA as an entity. In 1951, Walter Byers was named executive director of the NCAA.[24] He oversaw exponential growth in the association's popularity through the signing of television rights to broadcast games, the creation of postseason sporting events, and other events that allowed for increased exposure.

By the early 1960s, the NCAA was a household name. College athletes were becoming just as popular as professional athletes, but they were not receiving similar compensation. Instead, student-athletes received scholarships that paid for their educational experience. However, Byers believed that more distinct measures would suffice. He developed the term "student-athlete" in 1964 as a way to keep these students on an amateur status while preventing them from receiving workers' compensation for sport-related injuries. This term would plague athletes for decades. Although several student-athletes tried to sue the NCAA for its regulations on athlete compensation, few were successful in winning their cases. One of the more high-profile cases featured former college basketball player Ed O'Bannon.

In 2009, O'Bannon filed a lawsuit against the NCAA and the Collegiate Licensing Company (CLC) for violating antitrust laws that banned him from profiting off of his image. His image was featured in the Electronic Arts (EA) Sports video game *NCAA Basketball 09*. Several high-profile athletes including former NBA players Oscar Robertson and Bill Russell joined O'Bannon in their declaration that the NCAA violated rulings associated with the Sherman Antitrust Act. His lawsuit faced years of roadblocks until California District Court judge Claudia Wilken intervened.

On August 8, 2014, Judge Wilken ruled in favor of O'Bannon, citing that the NCAA did violate antitrust law. Moreover, Wilken ordered the NCAA to pay the plaintiffs in the case nearly $43 million in fees and costs. The CLC, which held licensing agreements with over two hundred universities, and EA settled out of court with their own $40 million payouts, which were equally distributed to nearly one hundred thousand student-athletes who had appeared in EA's football and basketball video game franchises. This set a precedent for policy changes regarding the amateur status of college athletes.

Five years later, California senators Nancy Skinner, Scott Wilk, and Steven Bradford presented a proposal to the state senate that would allow student-athletes within the state to legally sign endorsement and sponsorship deals based on their name, image, and likeness (NIL). On May 22, 2019, the senate voted in favor of the statute 31–5, with the California Assembly unanimously voting in favor of it on September 11, 2019.[25] Officially dubbed the "Fair Pay to Play Act" (FPPA), California governor Gavin Newsome officially signed the statute into law on September 30, 2019. In a statement released via Twitter and LeBron James's cable television series *The Uninterrupted*, Governor Newsome explained that "colleges reap billions from student-athletes but block them from earning a single dollar. That's a bankrupt model."

The premise of the FPPA is not that universities will be forced to compensate student-athletes for their performances in the field of play. Rather, student-athletes would be able to hire agents or other legal representation that would represent them in acquiring sponsorships or other endorsement deals. Shortly after the FPPA was made into law, many state lawmakers introduced similar legislation. For example, South Carolina introduced a bill that allowed the state's largest institutions to pay $5,000 stipends to football and men's basketball players, along with allowing the players to earn money from autographs and sponsorships. In New York, a state senator introduced the first bill that extends the FPPA to require colleges to pay student-athletes directly.

By the end of 2020, over forty state representatives had introduced legislation seeking equality for student-athletes. While there was overwhelming support for such legislation, there were still detractors. Leaders of the Pac-12, the governing body of college sports on the West Coast, expressed that passage of the FPPA will have negative consequences that blur the lines on how athletes can be recruited and what are deemed professional versus amateur sports. The NCAA also warned against negative ramifications that would make professional sport and amateur sport indistinguishable. However, the association promised to make reforms that would relax rules that prohibited compensation.

With the NCAA watching its power diminish, they made one final appeal to the Supreme Court hoping to revise the O'Bannon ruling from 2014. The Supreme Court obliged and accepted their appeal. They consolidated the appeal with the *American Athletic Conference v. Alston* case and held the same official argument as in *National Collegiate Athletic Association v. Alston* on March 31, 2021. On June 21, 2021, the Supreme Court unanimously voted to uphold the O'Bannon case, in which it previously ruled that the NCAA violated antitrust laws.

Consequently, NIL was made into law across the United States. Under this law, all athletes can receive compensation through endorsements and sponsorships based on their public persona. This ruling has forced the NCAA to amend its rules and has provided an avenue for lawmakers to question the power of the association as college athletics' major governing body. Lastly, this ruling has established a platform for Black athletes who have perceivably been exploited by the NCAA to enjoy the benefits of their labor.

In their mission to help Black college athletes in their quest for equality, the Knight Commission on Intercollegiate Athletics developed a strategic plan. According to the commission's website, the plan has four components:

1. *Closing educational opportunity gaps to create equitable pathways for Black college athletes' success during and after college.* These recommendations include permanently eliminating standardized test scores as an athletics eligibility criterion and instead employing a more holistic review of student readiness. (The NCAA currently is reviewing the use of standardized testing for determining eligibility and suspended the use of test scores for three years due to the pandemic.) The report also calls for the NCAA to dramatically boost financial support for historically Black colleges and universities (HBCUs) in the Accelerating Academic Success Program.
2. *Holding institutions accountable in recruitment and hiring to achieve diversity and equity in athletics leadership.* Among other recommendations, the report urges conferences and schools to adopt the "Russell Rule" as standard practice (named in honor of Bill Russell and first adopted by the

West Coast Conference). The Russell Rule requires each institution to include a member of a traditionally underrepresented community in the pool of final candidates for athletics leadership positions, including athletic director and head coach. Each conference school and the conference office would file an annual report card on the demographics of athletic leadership searches and hiring.

3. *Investing in programs that support and enhance Black athletes' college experience and promote inclusion and belonging.* Schools and conferences should be establishing a network of Black alumni and faculty to serve as mentors and providing a dedicated stream of funding for summer bridge programs for incoming Black college athletes.

4. *Creating more equitable opportunities for Black college athletes to assume leadership roles, especially in advocacy and governance.* Reforms should include establishing mentorship programs outside of the athletics department that enriches the development of Black athletes and expanding the ranks of college representatives who serve as advocates for the experiences of Black athletes. The report also calls for a safe process for Black athletes to report any discrimination or treatment concerns, without fear of reprisal.[26]

WE AREN'T FREE UNTIL YOU ACKNOWLEDGE IT

When Texas governor Greg Abbott signed the Sandra Bland Act into law in 2017, athlete activists and other supporters of BLM considered it a step in the right direction regarding establishing better protocols for inmates with mental health issues. The act, which mandates that county jails provide treatment for people with mental health challenges, was the first step in creating substantial changes within the criminal justice system. But many believed that there was more to dismantle. This belief came with the call to formally recognize the BLM movement as crucial in creating a better society.

Washington, DC, became one of the first cities to establish a monument dedicated to BLM. On June 5, 2020, Mayor Muriel Bowser teamed up with the DC Department of Public Works to paint "Black Lives Matter" in thirty-five-foot-tall yellow letters on a two-block section of Sixteenth Street NW near the White House. Further, Mayor Bowser officially renamed the section Black Lives Matter Plaza. With this monument being in the nation's capital, it represented the legitimacy of BLM as a call for the country to recognize social injustices against Black people.

Up to this point, the notion behind activism was that racialized incidents within society represent America's inherent history of treating Black individuals as less than. As mentioned in chapter 1, the midway point of the American Civil War represented the announcement of President Lincoln's Emancipation Proclamation. However, it was not until June 19, 1865, that Union soldiers arrived in Galveston, Texas, to announce that the nearly three hundred thousand slaves within the state were free. Colloquially known as "Juneteenth," it became a nationwide summer celebration that honored the sacrifices of those enslaved within the United States. But Black athletes were wanting more.

Cincinnati Bengals tackle Mike Daniels wrote an article in the *Players' Tribune* discussing the necessity of Juneteenth and what the movement meant for his family. Specifically, he described how Juneteenth was not something that was taught to him while growing up. He also said that he believes that many people from the Black community were as unaware of what the celebration meant as he was. He finished the article by urging lawmakers and other organizations to acknowledge Juneteenth as a federal holiday.

President Joe Biden agreed with these sentiments when on June 17, 2021, he signed the Juneteenth National Independence Day Act into law. This act officially made Juneteenth a federal holiday. Several athletes, including LeBron James, Kareem Abdul-Jabbar, and Nneka Ogwumike, praised the holiday but also warned that action must continue to recognize and eradicate racial injustice. This move further cemented the legacy of African American resilience throughout the United States. Now the movement was ready to go global.

As mentioned, BLM started as a simple tweet, but it morphed into a global movement. The UEFA European Football Championship, or simply known as the Euros, is one of the most popular soccer events in the world. Since 1958, these championships have been hosted every four years in the even-numbered years so as not to clash with the FIFA World Cup games. Known as a tournament that brings the world's best athletes together for fierce competition, racism would once again rear its ugly head.

Since the pandemic postponed 2020 sporting events, the Euro 2020 Championship was held in 2021. The final match was between England and Italy. The game was close during the entire match until it came down to the last shot attempt. Bukayo Saka, a Black Englishman and one of the youngest footballers to ever play in the championship, represented England in his shot attempt. Hit shot was blocked by the opposing team's goalie, and Italy would win the championship. While the loss was disappointing for England, this would not be the most egregious of emotions displayed.

Saka, along with other Black teammates, would receive death threats and have racial slurs hurled at them via social media. One Twitter post read, "Three fucking niggers missed! Stick BLM up my arse!" Another Twitter post said, "Lol here's the 'Englishmen' who blew it for England #ENGvsITA #EuroCup2021," while also posting a picture of Saka. The Football Association, the governing body for soccer in England, condemned those who hurled vitriol toward Saka and his teammates. These events were in addition to fans booing players throughout the championship who took a knee to protest global racial injustice. But the events that took place still show that racism in sport is not just a U.S. problem.

A MOVEMENT OF OLYMPIAN PROPORTIONS

The momentum of the 2020 athlete activism protests carried over into 2021 as athletes and other supporters of the BLM movement grew restless over the insufficient progress policy reform was making. While they continued to call out governments and organizations, the International Olympic Committee (IOC) worked to steer clear of political demonstrations. The last major political demonstration during the Olympics was the 1968 protests by John Carlos and Tommie Smith. They also received support from Australian track and field silver medalist Peter Norman, who shared the podium stage during the protest. Carlos and Smith were banned from further competition and from the Olympic Village as a result of the protests. Once they arrived home, they received further criticism, including death threats and negative media attention. Norman was ostracized by the Australian government and also received negative media attention.

To thwart future demonstrations, the IOC developed a set of rules that would help establish an apolitical platform for the Olympic Games. In 1975, the IOC officially established Rule 55. Under this rule, "every kind of demonstration or propaganda, whether political, religious, or racial, in the Olympics is forbidden."[27] Since its inception, the ruling has gone through several iterations. Most notably, Rule 50 would usurp Rule 55 as the most utilized defense against demonstrations. With Rule 50, "no kind of demonstration or political, religious, or racial propaganda is permitted in any Olympic sites, venues or other areas."[28] The Tokyo Olympics would challenge this ruling.

The 2020 Tokyo Olympics Games were one of several casualties of the COVID-19 pandemic. As a result of global shutdowns focusing on health and safety protocols, the games were postponed indefinitely. Following global rollouts of vaccinations that aided in suppressing symptoms of the virus, the IOC decided to reconvene to hold the Summer Games in 2021. Japanese citizens were not as eager as the IOC to continue the games, as a number of them gathered in large crowds to protest the games. Mounting concerns regarding the lack of vaccines and perceptions of insufficient safety protocols were some of the more pressing reasons for the protests. The Japanese automaker Toyota Motor Corporation decided that it would not broadcast television commercials domestically as it was worried about reputation management. In addition to citizen protests, American athletes were gearing up for protests of their own.

On the 2019 Pan American Games stage in Lima, Peru, US competitors Gwen Berry and Race Imboden raised a fist and took a knee respectively in support of the BLM movement. This caused the IOC to issue yearlong probations to the two athletes along with warnings to those who would participate in the 2020 games that such actions would not be tolerated. But after the killings of Breonna Taylor and George Floyd, followed by the subsequent protests of athlete activists, the IOC had to reconsider their ruling.

The U.S. Olympic and Paralympic Committee, which is the committee charged with overseeing the protection and support of American athletes, initially intervened by relaxing the sanctions incurred for those who engage in political protests. The IOC simultaneously explored how they could amend Rule 50 by sending out a survey to athletes across the globe on whether they should be allowed to engage in protests. After several athletes reported that they were in favor of Rule 50, the IOC upheld the overall premise of the rule while making a small change: athletes could express their views before a competition or during the player/team introductions. But they could not engage in podium demonstrations. While this represented the first major reform of policy regarding political demonstrations in global sport, many were still not satisfied.

As word spread about the IOC reinforcing Rule 50, a group of signatories decided to take action. Led by organizations including the Muhammad Ali Center, the Australia Human Rights Institute, Global Athlete, Athlete Ally, and the Olympism Project, more than 150 experts across five continents signed an open letter to the IOC denouncing Rule 50. Particularly, they suggested that the IOC should revise its protocols to meet human rights standards. Still, the rule was not explicitly eradicated.

As the 2020 Olympic Games commenced, several athletes engaged in protests before, during, and after competitions. Luciana Alvarado, who is the first gymnast from Costa Rica to qualify for the Olympic Games, ended her floor routine by taking a knee and holding up her fist in support of the BLM movement. NBC News reported that her demonstration was the first of its kind on the international stage in a gymnastics competition. British soccer player Nikita Parris took a knee and held up her fist before her team's match with Japan in solidarity with the BLM movement. This prompted several women's soccer players from various teams to engage in the same gesture.

Mental health among athletes became another point of emphasis as the Olympic Games continued. Multiple gold medal–winning gymnast Simone Biles suspended her competition, citing concerns for her mental health and the unexpected death of her aunt. She received worldwide support from fans and other athletes alike. Biles would later explain that her previous sexual abuse situation at the hands of former USA Gymnastics doctor Larry Nassar was another complication that proved to be challenging as she was preparing for the games.

U.S. shot-putter Raven Saunders earned a silver medal in the shot-put competition. She engaged in a political demonstration reminiscent of Smith and Carlos.[29] During her podium celebration, Sanders raised her arms above her head forming an X symbol by crossing her wrists. She would say that the symbol represented "the intersection of where all people who are oppressed meet."[30] The IOC launched an investigation into the demonstration as it violated Rule 50. Shortly after, they dropped the investigation in respect to Saunders, whose mom passed away two days after her silver medal celebration. After this, Saunders took a break from the media to concentrate on her mental health.

The conclusion of the Tokyo Olympic Games not only showcased a world that was ready to move past pandemic protocols. It was also one that showcased the power of athlete activism as it reached the global stage. Future Olympic host countries must now continue to amend their rules as the athletes have now recognized their power to hold organizations accountable for not being better for society.

Chapter Five

The Sport Justice Movement

With the state of global politics remaining volatile, it begs the question: will we ever reach a point where social justice is attainable? While the answer to this remains uncertain, the court of public opinion has continued to be a staunch proponent of holding those in power accountable for their various unethical actions. Technological innovations (e.g., social media, online streaming) have created a more immediate global society, which also increases the power of everyday citizens to voice their opinions and concerns. Likewise, the world of sports has been central in the goal of creating a more just global society.

What is being recognized now is that Black athlete activism in the age of Black Lives Matter (BLM) has shown a vigor like never before to create substantial changes in the policies that currently affect the goals of true social change. In speaking with current and former athletes, lawyers, scholars, and allies to the cause, it is clear that the new movement has availed itself to the needs and wants of athletes who are trying to create a more just society. In what I call the sport justice movement (SJM), we are in a new era of understanding the role of activism not only from the athletes' perspective, but also in their collaborations with their employers, outside organizations, and everyday citizens. To understand the SJM, we must first understand where it derives from.

ORGANIZATIONAL JUSTICE

As mentioned in chapter 4, the sports world protests reached a pinnacle when the Milwaukee Bucks decided to sit out their game-five matchups against the Orlando Magic in the 2020 Eastern Conference play-offs for the police shooting of Jacob Blake. While controversial, it sparked a league-wide conversation regarding how both the league and its players should handle social justice issues. The players, owners, and league administrators devised a plan to curtail players sitting out games by developing initiatives and in-game procedures that specifically addressed concerns regarding police brutality and other injustices against Black people. This was a move that is known in the scholarly world as organizational justice.

The civil rights movement sparked a shift in the ways that minorities were treated in the United States. Leaders in the movement fought for equality, equity, and their rights for integration. This movement also spawned a shift in how organizations operated. Starting in the early 1960s, scholars began to create theoretical frameworks that sought to understand the role of equity in the workplace. The initial pieces of this work were through equity theory, which was created by psychologist John Stacey Adams to understand how perceptions of equal pay versus nonequal pay would affect employees in the workplace.

More so, Adams identified four specific keys to recognizing inequity in the workplace.[1] They were (1) perceived inequity creates tension in an individual, (2) the amount of tension is proportional to the magnitude of the inequity, (3) this created tension motivates the individual to reduce it, and (4) the strength of the motivation to reduce the inequity is proportional to the perceived inequity. In other words, the perception of inequity in the workplace determines the action that the employee takes to correct the issue.

What is known is that during the time this theory was created, the workplace was not an equitable place in terms of pay. But for Black people, equal pay was not the only issue. Promotions, lack of opportunity, and mistreatment in the workplace remained rampant. While the progression of justice in the workplace was not the sole cause of the issues that Black people faced, the Black leaders within the civil rights movement were the catalyst to organizational change for all who perceived unfairness in the workspace.

Thus, organizational justice can be considered a framework of business ethics that identifies the necessity for organizations to treat employees fairly and act as just members of the society in which they belong. The initial concerns of organizations under Adams and his theory were first described under the concept of distributive justice. This form of organizational justice described how employees perceived the outcome of a situation as fair. For example, if a company hands out merit bonuses to employees of equal rank who have equally helped the company prosper based on annual reports, yet one employee receives less money than the other, this can be perceived as a violation of distributive justice.

Soon, however, employees began to question not only the way distributive justice was managed but also the rules and regulations that determined fairness outcomes as a whole. Scholars began to address this by examining the processes in which organizational leaders made decisions on fairness. This is called procedural justice.[2]

Psychologist Gerald Leventhal developed this understanding of justice by suggesting six keys to success. They are that procedures should (1) be applied consistently across people and across time, (2) be free from bias, (3) ensure that accurate information is collected and used in making decisions, (4) have some mechanism to correct flawed or inaccurate decisions, (5) conform to personal or prevailing standards of ethics or morality, and (6) ensure that the opinions of various groups affected by the decisions have been taken into account.[3] What can be added to this perspective is that employees are also wanting a seat at the table when it comes to the development of procedures that promote justice. Thus, how willing are organizational leaders when it comes to letting employees sit in on board meetings that usually have major implications on key decisions that are turned into organizational policy?

While distributive and procedural justice were the dominant areas of examination under the organizational justice umbrella, a new aspect of the concept began to take shape. Not only were the procedures regarding fairness within organizations under scrutiny, but *how these procedures were disseminated to employees* became just as important. Specifically, how the employees perceived these messages was of prime concern. As such, business professor Robert Bies went on to explain this concept as interactional justice. He would go on to describe this level of justice as the notion that organizational leaders will be judged not only by the way they treat their employees in disseminating procedures on fairness but how they explain why such procedures were implemented in the first place. Taken together, organizational justice has been long used to understand how decisions on fairness made by organizational leaders affect an employee's job satisfaction, loyalty, trust, commitment, and behavior within and outside of that organization. However, the world of sport has introduced a new way of considering aspects of justice.

THE SPORT JUSTICE MOVEMENT

Within the last decade, the Black Lives Matter movement has galvanized athletes to take action on various social causes. What began as a crusade against police brutality has now morphed into the eradication of inequity both in the workplace and in society at large. What has been a glaring notion for this cause is that athletes have challenged the commissioners of their leagues, team owners, and other organizations that partner with sports organizations to help end social injustices. To this end, Black athletes have helped in developing a platform in the sport justice movement.

True to the concept of organizational justice, sport justice derives from the notion that athletes (the employees) and team owners/sports commissioners/coaches (the employers) should work cohesively to ensure fairness within the organizational structure. There is a clear employer/employee relationship between these parties. Also, athlete unions, at least in professional sports, have been created to help negotiate procedures implemented by administrators.

Where the SJM deviates from organizational justice is multifaceted. First, while many athletes are in someone's employ, they are often individually recognized as their brand. Professional athletes have enjoyed this status for over thirty years. The 2021 name, image, and likeness (NIL) ruling by the Supreme Court has now guaranteed that college athletes can receive compensation off their brands as well. This brand recognition is often derived from an athlete's reputation among fans and nonfans alike, regardless of whether or not they are liked.

CENTRAL TENETS OF THE MOVEMENT

Outside of the fields of competition and entertainment, sport has become a global platform for sustainable change. Athletes, politicians, nongovernmental organizations (NGOs), for-profit organizations, and various other entities have all convened throughout history to determine the best paths for providing basic human rights. As mentioned in chapter 1, initially liberation for Black people meant escaping from European imperialistic rule with an overall idea of expatriation back to Africa. Throughout the century, the ideas shifted to integration, equal rights, and equitable opportunities.

Most recently, many of the ideas about equality, equity, and freedom have taken their cues from the civil rights movement. Despite the dormancy of athlete activism from the 1980s to the 2000s, today's athletes have revolutionized sport as a legitimate avenue for seeking policy reform for years to come. So much so, that the United Nations, the global hub for peace relations, has declared sport a central component to its Agenda for Sustainable Development, a global initiative that seeks to eradicate various social ills that are a detriment to human existence. In their plans for peace, the UN has laid out six specific ways in which sport can be utilized. It can

1. ensure healthy lives and promote well-being for all at all ages;
2. ensure inclusive and quality education for all and promote lifelong learning;
3. achieve gender equality and empower all women and girls;
4. make cities inclusive, safe, and sustainable;
5. promote just, peaceful, and inclusive societies; and
6. revitalize the global partnership for sustainable development.[4]

While these components are admirable, they are not necessarily explicit. Questions remain as to how these components can be tangible. Additionally, in what ways can we measure the success of these components? While that is something to ponder, there is not a specific mention of timely issues such as police brutality against persons of color, harassment in the workplace, and other targeted issues that rear their heads daily.

What is clear is that the SJM has rallied around the Black Lives Matter movement to highlight particular social justice issues that require a more focused solution. As many of the athletes, civic leaders, scholars, and lawmakers discussed in this book have suggested, police brutality, equitable education opportunities, and community development, among other issues, are pertinent to the growth of Black people globally. Given this, here are the suggested tenets that can be used to articulate the purpose of the SJM:

1. *Sport not only has the power to change the world, but it also has the responsibility to do so.* During his address at the inaugural Laureus Sports Awards in 2000, former South African president Nelson Mandela uttered the words, "Sport has the power to change the world. . . . It is more powerful than governments in breaking down racial barriers and it laughs in the face of discrimination." Therefore, the connection between sport and politics should be considered advantageous to combat social ills.
2. *Athletes are not just entertainers; they are human as well.* Within the last decade, athletes have become adamant about protecting their mental health. The NBA became one of the first global sports organizations that have hired a sports psychologist dedicated to creating programs that seek to help athletes overcome issues such as anxiety and depression. As the Tokyo Olympics have shown as well, athletes are thankful that people from all over the world celebrate them in competition. However, they are recognizing that self-care and social causes that are important to them take precedence over the bottom-line agenda.
3. *Sports organizations and other affiliate organizations should remain collaborators in the fight against social justice.* What has made many aspects of the SJM successful is when coaches, commissioners, and sport apparel

organizations joined in the fight to combat social injustice. But the work must continue. Collaborative social justice efforts through sports need more than just a one-off donation or event. Collaborative social justice initiatives should be purpose driven and longitudinal, that is, backed by research gathered from the individuals for which the initiatives are purposed. Otherwise, it will remain lip service with no substance.

THE SPORT JUSTICE MOVEMENT IN ACTION

While the SJM has established itself as a platform that is here to stay, it is far from perfect. Any form of legislation created or presented by lawmakers when it comes to social reform takes time. So, introducing legislation by athletes or social justice organizations on behalf of athletes can take even longer. As this book comes to a close, it is imperative to understand where the SJM has made progress and where it has room for improvement.

Thus, athletes, scholars, lawmakers, and leaders of social justice organizations were interviewed to discuss the successes, challenges, and future for changing society through sport. Additionally, they were asked to address how the BLM movement has been instrumental in helping athletes create a movement of their own. Overall, many of these individuals were excited about the progress that sport has made by calling out lawmakers and organizational leaders in being supportive of social causes. However, laws such as the George Floyd Act and the John Lewis Act have been introduced but have yet to be passed despite advocacy from several high-profile athletes. Still, their beliefs in the intersection of sport and politics as a platform for tangible social change remain firm.

One of the leaders interviewed for this book was Nick Turner. Mr. Turner serves as the president and director for the Vera Institute of Justice.[5] In this role, he and his staff work to ensure fairness and equity in a justice system that has an exorbitant number of marginalized individuals as inmates. One of their most recent projects was in partnership with the NFL to help advance solutions for police-community relations via several public service announcements.

In understanding Vera's ongoing mission in using sport as a platform for social change, he explained that Colin Kaepernick and LeBron James are high-profile figures that were key in illuminating the sport's role in creating a better society. He said that former NFL player Justin Tuck and former NBA player and current Miami Heat assistant coach Caron Butler sit on Vera's board. Particularly, he would mention that Caron has worked on many initiatives in the state of Connecticut where he played basketball for the University of Connecticut. Further, Vera would aid Caron in helping to eliminate solitary confinement in the Connecticut prison system.

Mr. Turner also described various other partnerships that he has established with athletes and sports organizations via Vera's initiatives. For example, they partnered with the NBA and their NBA Cares Foundation on a youth development initiative. With the initiative, Vera facilitated workshops dedicated to educational empowerment. They also work to eradicate juvenile delinquency and recidivism by taking the youth to Rikers Island. Here, the youth discuss law enforcement procedures and ways in which officers can build better relationships with their communities.

In discussing how the BLM movement has helped athlete activism, he said that it is a profound, important, and necessary force for social change. He explained that it is not a terrorist organization like detractors claim it is. Rather, it is a welcome movement that places racial equity in the current global vernacular, and there is a cost for ignoring the lives of people who benefit from the movement. Relative to where athletes should go from here, Mr. Turner said that changing policies that positively transform society are a product of democracy. Therefore, he said athletes should continue to educate themselves by understanding the procedures behind policy reform.

Another leader that was interviewed was Jacques McClendon. Mr. McClendon is a former professional NFL player and current director of football affairs for the Los Angeles Rams. In his current role, he serves as the liaison between different departments and entities for the LA Rams. Mr. McClendon focused on how athlete activism is imperative to uplifting the Black community from which many of the players come. More so, he said that sport and politics are never going to be separated. But he also said that the politics between athletes, organizations, and legislators is often hard to navigate.

Despite this, he also explained that Los Angeles represents a very unique environment for developing, revising, and implementing their social responsibility initiatives due to the city's multicultural, multiethnic communities. He said that the LA Rams have formed numerous partnerships with different entities to move things forward in this space. This work is championed by the vice president of community affairs, Molly Higgins, and the director of social justice and football development, Jonathan Franklin.

Through one particular partnership, they have developed the Rise with the Rams program, which pairs children from affluent and nonaffluent backgrounds so that they can learn from each other to create a more equitable future. Additionally, he has worked out a partnership with the Watts unit of the Los Angeles Police Department (LAPD) to help them coach youth football league. Through this partnership, their hope is to help build positive relationships between the police and youth.

Another project that the Rams have worked on is in partnership with the Opportunity House, which is a Los Angeles–based nonprofit geared to help ensure sustainable living for community college students suffering from housing insecurity. Through this platform, students are able to have better opportunities to finish their degrees. He would also mention that as an African American leader within the front office of a major sport organization, he is incredibly grateful for the team listening to diverse members within the organization when they make decisions on the best ways the Rams can impact the community.

In discussing the successes and challenges of the Rams' programs, Mr. McClendon discussed how the most important goal in using sport to better society is one in which he seeks transformational and not transactional change. He says that while there has been a change with a few of the underserved youth who go through their programs, it takes time to see significant progress. Lastly, he would say that one of the biggest challenges relative to substantial progress with the programs is bandwidth.

The murder of George Floyd has transformed the work that the Rams and the NFL do. Mr. McClendon also focused on how the moment should become a movement. We should understand the inadequate ways in which African Americans are treated in this country. Instead of just focusing on individuals, he would suggest that the NBA, WNBA, and NFL have been the most influential leagues in uplifting Black voices in their social justice efforts.

In determining how much progress has been made with the SJM, he stated that the Rooney Rule in the NFL and the Bill Russell rule in the West Coast Conference are steps in the right direction. Both rules were established to increase diversity and inclusion. He said that progress has been made, but more is needed. His thoughts on how the SJM can flourish are that supporters must put in the work consistently and stay committed for true social change to be made.

As student-athletes have made strides in their quest for equitable and fair practices on the college campus, it was imperative to gain their insights into social justice. Thus, the next perspective is from Bel Rolley. Ms. Rolley is a soccer player from the University of Southern California (USC). She is also president of the United Black Student-Athletes Association (UBSAA), which is a national student-led organization based at USC that is dedicated to using the platform of sport to speak out on issues such as BLM, police brutality, and student-athlete well-being.[6] Since taking the helm as president of UBSAA in 2020, she found inspiration in Colin Kaepernick's national anthem protest. More so, she said that there cannot be any slacking regarding sport and social change.

Ms. Rolley did not expect much of the media attention that she and members of the association, college administration, staff, and other student-athletes received when they began demonstrating after the death of George Floyd. However, she mentioned that their call for social justice on the college campus inspired other universities across the nation to form their own associations that ensured the well-being of Black student-athletes.

She explained that some of the early success of UBSAA was that sixty student-athletes from various sports across USC's campus immediately joined after the formal founding of the organization. One of their top priorities was to advocate for more Black psychologists and athletic trainers that would help them with recovery and mental health. She also said that BLM is more than just a hashtag and that it means everything to her as she pushes for equality and the eradication of oppression throughout the college experience. When she and her teammates wore BLM T-shirts at various competitions and social events, the team lost over one thousand followers. But they believed in the mission of Kaepernick and advocated for more administrative support in their quest to make true social change.

One of the largest policy shifts that Ms. Rolley focused on was the formation of the BLM action team. This action team, which was formed by USC athletics, works to increase scholarships for Black athletes not on full scholarship and to make a push for more Black student-athletes to amplify their voices on injustices on and off campus. What she sees as the best way to move forward is for college athletes to be allowed to express themselves freely regarding issues that matter to them without the fear of being penalized. She ended her interview by saying that college campuses have a long way to go in supporting athletes because social issues are multifaceted. But she believes that organizations similar to the UBSAA that are growing across other college campuses are a promising start to a better society.

For legislators to fight for social change, it takes careful and thorough empirical research. That is, understanding how societal shifts influence human behavior happens through research studies that can explain and oftentimes predict how people will make future decisions. Given this, how athlete activism affects true social change can be best explained by scholars who examine such phenomena. The scholar interviewed for this understanding was Dr. Joseph Cooper. Dr. Cooper is the J. Keith Motley Chair of Sports Leadership and Administration at the University of Massachusetts–Boston (UMass-Boston). He is a globally renowned expert whose work focuses on the intersection between sport, education, race, and culture, with an emphasis on sports involvement as a catalyst for holistic development.

Dr. Cooper said that sport and politics are forever intertwined. He said there is no such thing as being apolitical. Further, he said that if you are silent, that is political. Educational rights, labor rights, and other human rights are all political. Also, he said that there is a heightened level of consciousness through sport, and everyone has the power to activate a movement. He would end his thoughts on sport and politics by suggesting that those who are involved should focus on what aims are being met and who is benefiting from the results.

While not exclusively creating a new policy, Dr. Cooper has used his research to assist several organizations in understanding sport's role in making tangible social change. For example, he worked with the Muhammad Ali Center in Louisville, Kentucky, to strengthen advocacy for grassroots organizations. Also, he focuses on his membership in several nationally recognized scholarly associations including the North American Society for Sport Management, the American Education Research Association task force on education and sport, and the College Sport Research Institute. At his university, he serves as the cochair for the UMass-Boston restorative justice initiative. Through these scholarly organizations and his role at his university, Dr. Cooper has created new knowledge that advocates for reform through the power of sport.

While on the college campus, Dr. Cooper also advocates for equity and consciousness for students who are not familiar with the Black plight but want to gain an understanding. Particularly, he explains that BLM is grounded in a humanistic philosophy that Black people are human beings. Also, he believes that social media has expedited the understanding of the lived experiences Black people face every day. However, he explained that using the Black boys' and men's deaths as rallying cries while also seeing a lack of Black male leadership in the movement is problematic. Still, he says there are strengths to the movement that have catalyzed the revitalization of the Black athlete activist.

Dr. Cooper focuses on many of the female athletes as leaders of the SJM. While he mentioned well-known athletes such as Colin Kaepernick, LeBron James, Bill Russell, and Kareem Abdul-Jabbar, he says that Renee Montgomery and Maya Moore are vital in the movement because they voluntarily gave up their careers in the pursuit of justice. However, he says that while these are exemplar cases of social justice, he fails to see lasting change. Lastly, he cautioned that leaders and supporters of the new athlete activist movement should be open to change and constructive criticism.

Luke Fedlam was the final person interviewed for this book.[7] He is a partner and non-agent sports attorney for Porter Wright Morris & Arthur LLP based out of Columbus, Ohio. He is also the founder and CEO of the Anomaly Sports Group, which is a life skill and development firm for college and professional athletes. Mr. Fedlam has traveled extensively, educating many student-athletes and institutions on several topics such as NIL, contract analysis, immigration issues, asset protection, human rights issues, brand and market protection, and trust and estate protection.

Regarding sport and politics, Mr. Fedlam said it plays a significant role in society. He also said that these two intersections have the platform and ability to positively affect communities with initiatives that are important to athletes and sports organizations. He added that politicians often want to benefit from the celebrity status of athletes but also want them to "shut up and dribble" when it comes to speaking up against social injustices.

Relative to how his platform has been used to forward the SJM, Mr. Fedlam said that education and exposure are the keys to creating reform. Particularly, he works with student-athletes, their parents, administrators, coaches, and front offices in helping them understand their rights and avoid being taken advantage of by the legal system. He said that being a Black professional working with many high-profile Black athletes has been an added benefit due to the increased relationship building and trust that is developed. That is what he considers the highest level of success with the work he does. However, one of the main challenges is helping athletes at an early age understand the broader business side of sport, which will help them in life after sport. Many of these athletes want to engage in several social causes adjacent to and beyond their sports careers. Mr. Fedlam cautioned that navigating those waters can be murky.

Since the BLM movement commenced in 2013, Mr. Fedlam has seen a shift in the social causes and policies that have been triggered by key sports figures. However, he took a more personal approach to what the movement meant. He said that as a Black man with a ten-year-old son, the BLM movement means that he is valued as a human being. He also explained that BLM does not mean that Black lives are more important than any other life; it just means that Black lives should be equal to everyone else's life. Relative to how BLM has influenced athlete activism, he shared sentiments with Jacques McClendon in that there cannot be one single athlete who takes the credit for moving society forward. Rather, he said that all Black and brown athletes who have called out organizations to be better for society should be lauded for their hard work. Lastly, he suggested that Renee Montgomery's decision to opt out of the 2020 NBA season is monumental to how sport and social justice have meshed together.

Regarding lasting policy reform, Mr. Fedlam stated that he has not seen major policy changes regarding social injustice but remains hopeful that the educational programs that he and other legal experts are disseminating will create tangible, sustainable change. He acknowledged the voting procedures that athletes have fought for, but the George Floyd Act has yet to be made into law. He said that if this act is made into law, it would be a substantial victory for lawmakers and athletes who advocated for it.

Relative to the future of the SJM, Mr. Fedlam explained that athletes should take the time to figure out what they are trying to do. He challenged athletes to ask themselves, what is the desired outcome? What change do they want to see? He suggested that once they educate themselves on how to get there, they should consider how they can be the most effective in creating change. More so, he said that whether it is awareness, allyship, legislation, or organizational policy, educate yourself. For example, he cautioned athletes not to schedule a march without understanding what permits are needed. Also, he suggested that if you want legislative change, understand current legislation. There will be obstacles and challenges, but as long as you set the goals, write the vision, and educate yourself, then you can have others come help you to address the issues.

MOVING FORWARD WITH SPORT JUSTICE

The SJM is primed to be the next wave of athlete activism and policy reform. Before the 2021 NFL season, former NFL player and ESPN analyst Ryan Clark praised the Tampa Bay Buccaneers on his Twitter account for having a diverse coaching staff. After posting this, several comments expressed that Clark and the NFL should not make things racial. Some could say that this was another attempt of individuals expressing the need for politics to stay out of sports. But as mentioned in chapter 1, these intersections have been intertwined for nearly 150 years.

As such, major U.S. sports organizations have been accused of not hiring minority candidates in executive or head coaching positions despite the fact that the two most popular U.S. sports organizations, the NFL and the NBA, have predominantly minority players. (A major lawsuit featuring former NFL head coach Brian Flores will be discussed later in this chapter.) To quell such assertions, some sports organizations have created protocols for the hiring and retention of minority candidates. For example, Dan Rooney, who was the former owner of the Pittsburgh Steelers, established the Rooney Rule in 2003.

Under this rule, the NFL required teams to interview minority candidates for executive and head coaching jobs. Considered an outlet of affirmative action, the rule only required teams to interview candidates, without a hiring preference or the requirement of meeting a quota. However, there remains a scarcity of head coaches and team executives across all U.S. professional sports. This would prompt one grassroots organizer to engage in a silent but worthwhile protest.

Lou Richie, an activist and organizer from Oakland, California, decided to engage in a peaceful protest during the 2021 Pac-12 basketball tournament to which he wanted to point out the lack of Black head coaches within the conference. To highlight this, Richie wore a T-shirt that said "Black Head Coaches Matter." His decision to protest was in large part due to the killing of George Floyd and issues such as voter suppression. Along with the organization Advancement of Blacks in Sports, which is a New York City grassroots basketball organization formed in 2020 after George Floyd's murder, Richie continues to work to secure positions for Black coaches.

THE FUTURE OF SPORT JUSTICE

Sport has been widely known to bring people together. Whether the combination of sport and politics has been met with praise or contempt, the combination has always led to differences of opinion on one or more specific phenomena. Globally, sports have been used for decades to bring about peace and development initiatives. For example, the 1995 Rugby World Cup was a watershed moment that, for a brief time, brought about discussions on community building among Black and white South Africans. It was the first sporting event to help in bridging the racial gap relative to the consequences of apartheid.

However, some have expressed that for every time sport has worked to contribute to dismantling social injustice, there are more times in which sport has contributed to ongoing issues in the forms of injustice that generally serve as microcosms of society. What the ongoing issues of social injustice coupled with the pandemic have shown our global society is that people who have consistently been marginalized are making a push for better social well-being. Within the context of sport, the SJM offers a pathway forward to challenge existing policies that deny and denigrate those who have dealt with all manners of prejudice and discrimination. As one article says,

> Sport is a human institution, a universal phenomenon that serves to instill a sense of belonging or meaning to many individuals' lives. Let us not place value on athletes, let us place value on the impact their profession has on humanity; the realization of athletes as commodities and sport as a political and pecuniary service will help reshape the perception that sport is merely a means of amusement and diversion from personal hardships. Our world can exist without the arrogance and egotism attributed to certain athletes, and it can surely exist without the barefaced disregard several sports organizations

have for their dedicated fan base. But, we may question whether or not this world can function without the hidden values embedded in competitors and the communal insight sports give us on a national scale.[8]

Given this, the last section of this book will highlight the impact that the SJM could have on the larger conversation regarding social justice.

SPORT JUSTICE AS A MECHANISM OF DIVERSITY, EQUITY, AND INCLUSION

Across all levels, sport has been perceived as a platform that offers equal opportunity. From the front office to the bleachers, sports have purportedly been the beacon of hope when it comes to establishing an inclusive society. But while this idea pervades the world of sport, there are still things that must change. One example pertains to a scandal involving NFL workplace hiring practices.

On February 1, 2022, former Miami Dolphins head coach Brian Flores filed a lawsuit against the NFL claiming racial discrimination. In his lawsuit, Flores claimed that Dolphins owner, Stephen Ross, tried to coerce him to lose games as a way to gain a high draft pick in the 2022 NFL draft. The reward for losing these games would have been financial compensation that would have been distributed for each loss. Additionally, Flores sued the New York Giants, Denver Broncos, and Houston Texans for a multitude of reasons, including setting up head coaching interviews despite not taking him seriously as a candidate and interviewing him even though the teams had already selected other coaches.

Several sports analysts and former NFL coaches supported Flores in his lawsuit. Many of the former coaches, who happen to be Black, would share similar stories of being coerced to purposefully lose games or of not getting the length of time to build their teams in comparison to their white counterparts. The lawsuit calls into question the relevancy of the Rooney Rule and similar initiatives on diversity, equity, and inclusion across all sports platforms. Within college sports, there are similar issues. Primarily, this controversy has focused on the continued exploitation of student-athletes. The ruling regarding student-athlete representation was no exception. On August 6, 2019, the NCAA announced that any agent who seeks to represent college basketball players as they navigate their NBA draft options must, among other criteria, have a bachelor's degree. This ruling prompted LeBron James and his agent, Rich Paul, to call out the NCAA for its alleged discriminatory and exploitative ruling.

Paul, who is a Black male and does not have a college degree, exposed that this ruling limits the platform for agents who come from lower socioeconomic backgrounds and those who have alternative career trajectories. However, James went further to express that the NCAA was specifically targeting Paul, ultimately dubbing the announcement as the "Rich Paul Rule."

Amid the backlash from Paul, James, and other sports figures, the NCAA decided to amend the rule to include agents without colleges degrees provided they are in good standing with the National Basketball Players Association (NBPA).

Although the NCAA's amendment of the rules provides a more inclusive platform regarding college basketball player representation, this latest flub speaks volumes to an already open call for the organization to reform its policies or succumb to them. The NCAA, a nonprofit organization that prides itself on being dedicated to the well-being and lifelong success of college athletes, has been staunchly criticized for generating over a billion dollars in revenue while college athletes remain unpaid beyond scholarships. Since 2006, high school basketball players were ineligible to jump straight into the NBA. Instead, they had to wait one year after their high school graduation to become draft eligible. This saw a rise in high school athletes playing one year of college basketball before declaring for the NBA draft. Dubbed as the "one-and-done" era, this ruling essentially controlled how student-athletes navigated their professional careers. However, the nuances of how funds are earned through tournaments such as March Madness have prompted student-athletes to take career matters into their own hands.

There has been a burgeoning trend of elite high school basketball players skipping college and playing professional basketball overseas before becoming eligible for the NBA draft. While the NCAA claims that their rules are there to protect current and future student-athletes, many counter that the rules restricting the eligibility of when high school players can enter the NBA draft are exploitive. Paul, who is one of those critics of the NCAA's "one-and-done" rule, is also spearheading the platform for high school athletes to find alternative paths to the draft. In 2018, former five-star basketball recruit Darius Bazley initially committed to Syracuse University before ultimately taking a year off in preparation for the 2019 NBA draft. During this time, Bazley signed with Paul's agency, Klutch Sports. With this deal in place, Bazley secured an internship at New Balance worth $1 million to gain insight into the business of sport. While Syracuse head basketball coach Jim Boeheim viewed Bazley's choice to decommit from the university as a mistake, Paul saw it as an empowerment tool for athletes who wish not to be used for their talents without compensation.

While Paul and others have expressed that receiving an education in college sports is of value, they insist that compensating student-athletes would prevent them from getting taken advantage of or breaking current NCAA rules. The NCAA recently settled on a $208 million lawsuit that declared that the organization could not restrict compensation to athletes regarding their education. The State of California passed the Fair Pay to Play Act, which changed the business model of the NCAA. However, current NCAA president Mark Emmert warned legislatures that if they were to approve the act, California schools could face the possibility of not participating in postseason play.

California state senators Nancy Skinner and Steven Bradford introduced this act because current NCAA rules remain heavily unfair to students from low-income communities and to female athletes who have fewer opportunities to play professional sports than men. California student-athletes are now eligible to sign contracts with several endorsers, including video game publishers, apparel companies, sporting good entities, and auto dealers. Still, the NCAA along with several California universities expressed that such a deal would not only confuse current student-athletes but would present a plethora of challenges to the collegiate sports model.

But the current collegiate sports model is what is negatively affecting current student-athletes, particularly African American males who participate in high-revenue-generating sports. While the NCAA scrambles to change rules that negatively affect student-athletes, agents such as Paul will continue to usher in a more dynamic approach to student-athlete empowerment that will eventually overshadow the more static rules the governing body of collegiate sport utilizes.

For Paul and other individuals who work to eradicate the current NCAA sports model, the rule changes on athlete compensation represent a chance for student-athletes to take control of their upward mobility. As the NCAA continues to take hits to its already fragile reputation in handling student-athlete exploitation, the trend for athletes to skip college altogether remains slow but steady. For the NCAA, the reputation for the future of the organization will rely heavily on how much they commit to the integrity of education and how much they amend their obsolete rules concerning perceived athlete exploitation.

Although the NBA leads all major sports leagues in diversity hiring practices, there is still a stark difference between the number of players versus the number of Black executives. Moreover, there remain only four Black executives above a general manager position in comparison to a league that has nearly 75 percent Black players. Michael Jordan, who won six championship rings with the Chicago Bulls and is arguably considered the best player in NBA history, had to wait patiently with his 2006 minority investment in the Charlotte Hornets franchise before purchasing full control of the team in 2010. This was also after he was let go by the Washington Wizards franchise after he felt that he was going to return as president of basketball operations upon retirement. He is the only Black owner of any sports team across all major sports. In 2018, the Dallas Mavericks named Cynthia Marshall as CEO of the franchise. She is the first Black female and first female CEO of an NBA franchise. Her first task as CEO of the team was to investigate allegations of sexual misconduct within the organization. Even Marshall's front-cover feature in *Bloomberg Businessweek* suggested that she was in charge of cleaning up a Me Too movement mess.

Despite this remarkable feat regarding Black executives in the NBA, there is still an uphill climb for representation. Systematic oppression has always been at the forefront of Black people breaking into the upper echelon of executive positions in corporate America. For those who have made it to the C-suite ranks, the problem is keeping them there. Further, problems loom from years of being passed over for promotions, having to deal with covert and overt racial slurs, and outgrowths of depression. Considering this, Johnson's claims of being "free as a bird" and "handcuffed" in a position where he was given full control speaks volumes to the hurdles Black sports executives face moving forward. Even though there is a small level of growth, developing a work culture that strives to retain Black sports executives should be the next order of business.

SPORT JUSTICE AS ENVIRONMENTAL AND COMMUNITY SUSTAINABILITY

In 2021, the Los Angeles Clippers announced that the team will be building a new arena in Inglewood, which is located in Los Angeles County. The arena would be officially titled Intuit Dome after the team signed a $500 million naming rights deal with the financial software company. Additionally, the Clippers teamed up with financial services firm Aspiration as a way to make the stadium more environmentally friendly. With their business offerings, "Aspiration allows its customers to choose how much they pay for banking services and espouses a mission of combating climate change—it promises, for instance, not to put any money into funding the coal or oil industries."[9]

Taken together, the Clippers are seeking to establish the first climate-positive arena with a commitment to be 100 percent carbon free when it opens its doors in 2024. Furthermore,

Intuit Dome will operate as a fully electric arena, and the Clippers said the complex would save nearly 10 million gallons of water per year through conservation and the use of reclaimed water. In addition, the complex will use carpool incentives that the Clippers claim could reduce vehicle trips by 15%, and help the Port of Los Angeles buy 26 electric tugboats to improve local air quality.[10]

Still, concerns loom regarding the community identity of the city.

Within the last five years, citizens of Inglewood have accepted the realization that their communities are going to change with the construction and eventual completion of a $5 billion sport and entertainment arena. First, SoFi Stadium became the host facility of both the Los Angeles Rams and the Los Angeles Chargers. The Intuit Dome, which will be the new home for the Los Angeles Clippers, will add to its growth as a sports hub. And the opening and closing ceremonies of the 2028 Olympic Games will be hosted in the city, as well. Those who have invested in the city during this time frame will certainly benefit from increases in the market value, but local citizens do not share the same sentiment. Several grassroots organizations along with local businesses were staunchly against this growth.[11]

While Inglewood used to be a predominantly Black city, it has now become predominantly Latino.[12] Still, many of the individuals within this demographic fear that all of the new development will cause an increase in gentrification. Construction within the city also caused fears of increased pollution and traffic congestion, which is already an ongoing issue in Los Angeles County. The need to keep the community intact is particularly important as only 9 percent of the population in the entirety of Los Angeles County is African American. Gentrification has forced many African Americans to move out of the area. Therefore, many of the longest-standing residents are left to cope with rising costs and loss of community.

Similarly, many individuals from marginalized communities have to adjust to the socioeconomic and environmental consequences of major sports organizations infiltrating their communities. For example, the Olympic Games are held in major cities across the globe. While many watch the spectacle that is associated with the opening and closing ceremonies of the Games, many marginalized individuals who live within the host cities often share a different story once the games end.

When the International Olympics Committee selected Rio as a host city in 2009, thousands of jubilant Brazilians crowded Copacabana Beach to celebrate. The Brazilian government voted to use the Olympics to solve long-existing problems, including a pledge to treat 80 percent of Rio's sewage. Most citizens seemed optimistic that the Games could ignite the local economy and clean up their city. Fast-forward to the current day, and exceedingly high crime rates, dilapidated buildings, and contaminated water remain a problem. The discrepancy between the grand promises of socioeconomic improvement and the reality on the ground in previous host cities is troublesome. Although host cities and countries must participate in revitalization plans, the IOC must help develop strategies of its own. From infrastructure woes to human rights violations, the IOC has a responsibility to focus on both the ethics and profits of conducting business.

Given the long-term detrimental effects of the Olympic Games in Rio, it's no surprise that Budapest, facing civil unrest and a lack of cohesion among its political parties, withdrew its bid for the 2024 games. That leaves Paris as the winner. For 2028, the LA committee points to the 1984 Summer Olympics—considered one of the most successful in the Games' history—as a baseline for success for netting the IOC $225 million by being the first to utilize television contracts to advertise the Games. With this track record, it is not unreasonable to assume that the 2028 Olympic Games will be financially lucrative both for the IOC and for LA itself. Additionally, traffic congestion and homelessness remain important issues that the LA committee must address for a successful bid. Only one point is clear: Los Angeles cannot afford to follow in the footsteps of the 2016 Rio games. The future of the Olympics is under scrutiny. Many have raised the issue of the IOC only focusing on profits without caring for the people. Also, a litany of negative news about the IOC has surfaced, including allegations that its members have accepted bribes in return for voting for host cities. Such accusations could permanently taint or, worse, eventually lead to the downfall of the Games in their entirety.

The IOC could gain buy-in from stakeholders—consumers of the Games, suppliers, sponsors, and other individuals who are directly affected by the Games—if it provides tangible evidence of the socioeconomic advantages the Games will have. As stated on their website, the IOC is committed to building a better world through sport. But if stakeholders perceive the IOC as complicit in acts of discrimination, then preestablished relationships could be severed and future relationship development stunted. The IOC must be willing to be transparent and adapt to organizational change if it is to contend with an interconnected globalized society. Organizations can no longer operate under a closed-system mentality in which they simply ignore or fail to respond to public criticism. Scandals and deception have often plagued the IOC's mission to promote sustainability awareness, capacity building, and far-reaching actions for environmental, social, and economic development across society. Therefore, the IOC must focus on restructuring its organization to meet stakeholder needs and generate positive social change.

Social responsibility has never been a requirement for an organization's bottom line, but an increasing number of businesses now recognize that it is important and are working to reorient their strategies to incorporate ethical concerns. Given the history of problems in the cities hosting the Olympic Games, the IOC must not derail its ethical decision-making processes in favor of profit. Otherwise, the IOC will continue to blemish their reputation, leading others to question the relevance of the Games.

SPORT JUSTICE AND YOUTH DEVELOPMENT

Sports organizations are rife with examples of how sport benefits youth development. These organizations usually have nonprofit arms that offer several services for youth based on the communities in which teams are located. For example, the NFL sponsors a youth health movement called NFL Play 60. Under this movement, they promote physical and mental well-being by encouraging youth to get active for sixty minutes a day. For fifteen years, the NFL and the American Heart Association have partnered in making this agenda a national movement.

The NBA sponsors a similar organization that focuses on youth development called NBA Cares. According to their website,

> NBA Cares is the league's global social responsibility program that builds on the NBA's mission of addressing important social issues in the U.S. and around the world. NBA Cares programs and participants have provided more than 5.8 million hours of hands-on service, created more than 1,650 places where kids and families can live, learn or play, and engaged more than 60 million youth in basketball programs in communities around the world. Internationally, NBA Cares has created more than 332 places where kids and families can live, learn, or play in 40 countries. NBA Cares works with nationally and internationally recognized youth-serving programs that support education, youth and family development, and health-related causes, including Boys & Girls Clubs of America, Vera Institute of Justice, Thurgood Marshall College Fund, UNICEF, Special Olympics, Share Our Strength, and GLSEN.[13]

Law enforcement organizations have also used sport as a way to help underserved youth. Within cities that have multiple sports organizations, law enforcement agencies often partner with these organizations to provide outlets for youth to stay out of trouble. For example, the LAPD, one of the most publicized law enforcement agencies in the United States, has partnered with several professional sports teams to help youth who require assistance.

According to a recent report regarding Angeleno youth, nearly seventy thousand youth fall into a category of high risk titled "disconnected youth." These are individuals between the ages of sixteen and twenty-four who are neither working nor are in school. Of the disconnected youth in Los Angeles, 23 percent are African American; 15 percent are LatinX; 13 percent are youth who are either mixed race, did not identify, or are other ethnicities; 8 percent are white; and 8 percent are Asian.[14] This report also suggested that these youth either leave school because of teen pregnancy, familial obligations, health issues, or just a sheer disconnect with school. Given this, it is understandable that there have been many issues of crime, homelessness, and mental health problems for Angeleno youth. But this is not just an LA issue. Most cities in which sports organizations are entrenched in their communities must evaluate and revise their programs to provide sustainable improvements to these individuals.

SPORT JUSTICE AS A GLOBAL BRIDGE BUILDER

The Tottenham community of London is considered one of the more diverse in the world. With approximately two hundred languages spoken by individuals of different ethnicities, religions, and socioeconomic backgrounds, Tottenham is an area that is steeped in unique and diverse cultures. However, issues such as gentrification, police brutality, dilapidated housing, organized gangs, and high crime have plagued the community.

Much of the recent tensions within Tottenham were sparked when an unarmed Black man, Mark Duggan, was shot by police following an arrest. Consequently, this incident sparked outrage, fire, and violence during a five-night riot in 2011. Since that time, tensions between locals and the city government have not ceased. Now that the local government has plans for massive regeneration of the community, which includes plans for a possible NFL franchise, ten thousand new homes, and five thousand new jobs by 2025, tensions among locals have increased.[15]

Individuals in the Latin community of Tottenham have expressed anger regarding the local government's plans to replace the Seven Sisters Market of North London, one of the largest Latin business areas in the city, with retail stores.[16] Further, individuals in the area have expressed how their voices have been silenced concerning whether their needs will be met in the regeneration efforts. Sport organizations have been entrenched in local communities for decades. In particular, these organizations have a history of liaising with local governments to positively impact their communities. However, research is lacking on the impact that sport social responsibility initiatives have on community development, as well as on how cities in turn utilize these initiatives for environmental safety, diversity and inclusion, and sustainability efforts.[17]

Recently, the NFL, in its hopes of expanding globally, announced a ten-year agreement with the Tottenham Hotspur Premier League club that would guarantee a minimum of two NFL games played each year. Regarding the partnership, Tottenham Hotspurs chairman Daniel Levy explained that "the socio-economic benefits this will bring to the area will be immense and demonstrates our commitment to the regeneration of this priority borough in London."[18] But there is little knowledge of how sports organizations positively impact communities.[19]

Since 2005, the NFL has hosted games outside the United States to increase the popularity of the sport across international borders. This slew of games has been titled the NFL International Series. After the launch of the series in Mexico City, most of the games have been played in London. Despite its growing popularity in other parts of the world, U.S. issues, such as the continued protest against racism and social injustices, may have the league questioning its global expansion efforts. Former San Francisco 49ers quarterback Colin Kaepernick became a topic of controversy when he decided to protest the U.S. national anthem during a preseason game in 2016. Since his initial protest, Kaepernick has either sat or kneeled during the national anthem for every game, gaining support from teammates, players from others teams, and individuals across the country.

As mentioned, the purpose of Kaepernick's protest was to give a voice to people of color, reasoning that if the United States continues to ignore issues of racism, then those inspired by his demonstration will continue to protest. The problems that Kaepernick has brought forth must not be ignored, and the United States must continue to work toward progress. For the NFL, the issues of race and politics have been a point of consternation because the league has yet to determine the best ways to address uprisings regarding racial injustice.

The UK, however, is facing numerous socioeconomic, racial, and political problems. If the NFL is looking to expand globally, it must first recognize racial tensions and political issues in the countries where it is seeking to establish new franchises, including the UK.

As it continues to explore this expansion, the NFL will face issues related to the political uprising of people tired of the status quo regarding race relations. Therefore, the organization must understand that effective communication and strategy are key to its global growth. The NFL should liaise with a member of Black Lives Matter UK (BLMUK) as a way to show unity in the effort to eradicate racial injustice. Following the 2016 shooting death of Chicago native Paul O'Neal at the hands of the police, BLMUK participated in its first protest to show solidarity to Black victims in the United States. Since this time, BLMUK has fought against injustices toward marginalized groups throughout the country. Some of the group's more recent protests include blockades of the M4 near the London airport, roads in Nottingham, and the A45 near Birmingham. Natalie Jeffers, a cofounder of BLMUK, explained that the protests stemmed from the exorbitant number of Black men killed or imprisoned by British police. In fact, according to a report by the Prison Reform Trust, Black Britons make up 10 percent of the prison population but only 2.8 percent of the general population. The NFL must engage in discussion with this group to ascertain the breadth and depth of social injustices toward marginalized groups in the UK. If it is successful in understanding and addressing these issues, then it could avoid future player uprisings that would deter future growth and could create an image of the NFL as a global organization indifferent to the rights of the people.

The UK's Brexit vote in 2020 could also impact the NFL's ability to successfully expand across the Atlantic. Although the NFL should bear in mind the direct economic ramifications of the UK's withdrawal from the European Union, it should consider the social injustice ramifications as well. Civil unrest could have direct ties to the economic growth of a business. More specifically, individuals may be more likely to withhold financial support from an organization that they do not perceive as engaging in corporate social responsibility. According to a report in the *Guardian*, hate crimes have increased 58 percent since the Brexit referendum passed. Additionally, it was mentioned in a report by the *London Post* that Black Britons were over 17 percent more likely to be stopped and searched than their non-Black counterparts. One glaring pattern in these hates crimes is that majority-white UK residents are telling nonwhite residents to go back to their countries of origin. The NFL must consider the history of racism pre- and post-Brexit. If it ignores the social issues that have been magnified by the Brexit vote, it could face protests from people tired of being used and abused by corporate entities that prey on the weak.

Furthermore, the NFL must be careful not to market the expansion in a way that would be perceived as imperialistic by UK citizens. Soccer and rugby are two of the most popular sports in the UK, and the NFL is highly aware of the need to develop football's popularity before its initial investment into the market. The expansion should not be seen as an effort to force U.S. culture on UK citizens. Therefore, the NFL must be as transparent as possible about the true purpose of establishing a franchise in London. Given the bewilderment that has followed the Brexit vote, citizens are not ready to become embroiled in another political war in which they perceive that their rights have been violated. Therefore, making sure individuals understand the benefits and challenges of establishing a football franchise within their borders is critical if the NFL wants to gain buy-in from UK citizens.

Finally, the NFL must gain an understanding of the complexities and communication patterns of globalization. Globalization is not a static construct but a dynamic one with constant ebbs and flows. Like other businesses, the NFL should focus primarily on the economic aspects of globalization. Its mission is to provide entertainment to its fans, but it still recognizes that for its value to grow significantly, its International Series must expand. Even if economic imperatives come first, the NFL must not ignore avenues of social globalization, such as the ways that cultures are now augmenting their voices through advanced communication platforms. Everyday citizens are no longer waiting for major media outlets to decide how the news is disseminated. Instead, individuals are taking matters into their own hands through the internet and other means to challenge, critique, and demand change. For the NFL, understanding social globalization means that it must take into account the turbulence and uncertainty in any country caused by shifting cultural and technological dynamics. By providing an open forum of communication for both the organization and individual stakeholders, the NFL can ensure that these people have a say in its efforts to address racial injustices and other social issues. This ethos should extend beyond just establishing a franchise in London, but in the near term, establishing and maintaining itself as an ally to UK citizens as they navigate the turbulence of social unrest will help the NFL find success in its global expansion.

The NBA, whose global presence is more established than most U.S.-based sports, has increased its presence even more by establishing the Basketball African League. Also called NBA Africa, its CEO Victor Williams said,

> Social responsibility has been an integral part of the NBA's youth development efforts on the continent for more than three decades. Following the establishment of the NBA Foundation and the National Basketball Social Justice Coalition in the U.S. and building on our broader efforts to help create a more equal and just society, the NBA and the BAL each look forward to deepening their engagements with partners, community leaders, and other stakeholders to advance gender equality and create a more inclusive economic environment in Africa.[20]

In establishing such global connections, those within the SJM should continue to understand the policy standards of global countries to make sure efforts create tangible social change initiatives.

SPORT JUSTICE AS A COMMUNITY DEVELOPMENT PLATFORM

In cities nationwide, policy makers and business developers typically convene to discuss the best ways to improve their cities. However, when these improvements are in the planning stages, individuals without power or influence are often left out of the decision-making process, so how can public-private partnerships enhance residents' engagement on community development issues? Exploring how to collaborate with residents about community development through the context of sports offers one way to do this.

Unique Features Help Create Positive Community Impacts

Sports organizations have been entrenched in many local communities for decades. In particular, these organizations have had a history of creating initiatives to positively impact their communities. Sports have six unique features:

1. media distribution and communication power;
2. youth appeal;
3. the capacity to deliver positive health benefits through efforts that include getting youth involved in sports activities and modeling healthy habits and the advantages of exercise for youngsters;
4. social interaction;
5. cultural integration—people from diverse cultures and communities share a common experience when attending and enjoying a sporting event, sitting next to each other and relating to each other in a more positive way than they might in another setting; and
6. the ability to promote awareness of environmental and sustainability issues—for example, when a new sports stadium is being planned, the city responds to residents' concerns about increased traffic congestion by taking action to mitigate these impacts, thus resulting in a net environmental improvement for the community. Such processes work best when local government, community members, and the sports organization collaborate.

Using major and minor league sports for community development initiatives holds promise for cities and can inform future efforts. Although these organizations have expressed a commitment to community development for all individuals, similar moves by corporations have often resulted in gentrification and the disenfranchisement of marginalized individuals.

Tips for Success

Consequently, it's imperative to understand the magnitude of sports for development initiatives concerning the connections of local governance, community development, and its importance in providing a voice to residents. Consider the following ways in which such collaboration can be successful.

Establish an infrastructure that recognizes all neighborhood constituents. Most community infrastructures are based on three specific stakeholders:

1. residents within a specific geographic space, their family, friends, and neighbors;
2. grassroots, community, and nonprofit organizations that are established to serve residents; and
3. local media outlets that target specific groups or areas.

Collectively, these stakeholders provide value and information to policy makers and corporations looking to establish a presence in communities. By telling their stories, these stakeholders often provide examples that offer a glimpse into the issues or opportunities faced daily.

Conducting thorough research as part of engaging constituents within communities is an essential activity for policy makers and business developers. This research typically includes a series of interviews, focus groups, and observations of the daily lives of individuals so that their needs will be taken into account in the community development process.

Provide safe zones for constituents to express themselves. Stakeholders communicating their concerns about their communities must have safe zones in which they feel comfortable expressing themselves. Communities, policy makers, and business developers must cultivate an understanding of the environmental, technological, health, and socioeconomic issues that affect residents of all income levels. It can be challenging for members of the community to share their concerns candidly, and encouraging them to do so requires extra effort on the part of policy makers and business developers.

Thus, it is essential to provide safe zones where all community members have an equal opportunity to have their voices heard. Safe spaces for expression in settings beyond city council meetings may help encourage community members to become more involved in the community development process.

Evaluating sports as an agent for social change. As mentioned, sports can bring together communities, provide a space for cultural integration, and help individuals engage in larger social issues. For example, the San Francisco Giants created a program titled Junior Giants Strike Out Violence as a platform to help adults and youth discuss ways to prevent gang violence and bullying within their local communities. In Southern California, the LA Galaxy Foundation (created by the Major League Soccer team LA Galaxy) hosts a variety of charitable events to increase educational awareness and improve the communities surrounding the StubHub Center stadium where the team plays its home games, approximately ten miles south of downtown Los Angeles.

Using sports as a community development mechanism is an often underused and overlooked process.

Sustaining the Benefits

Many local advocates are calling for organizations to engage in more socially responsible business practices. However, the concept of social responsibility is often too focused on the bottom line of the business rather than on the needs of the communities in which it operates. Various urban planning scholars suggest that organizations should focus on developing relationships with community members and policy makers as ways to mutually negotiate development initiatives and sustain the benefits of a community development project after it has been completed.

Suggestions for Local Officials

Considering that sports are a part of most communities, it makes sense for policy makers to explore the concept of using sports in conjunction with community development. Local government officials may want to consider:

- facilitating and improving community-based organizations' communication with stakeholders as a way to engage in collaborative community development;
- exploring innovative ways to bridge gaps among various community members; and
- collaborating with business developers and academic researchers on community development initiatives to obtain an accurate assessment of the needs of all community members and stakeholders.

By working together, policy makers and business leaders can gain better insight into the communities they serve. Connecting with researchers who can help them accurately articulate their strategic planning initiatives can aid in creating positive community-level social change. In addition, policy makers can use data-driven results involving community members to help identify and map out their socioeconomic and environmental needs as part of the strategic planning process. And finally, policy makers may want to consider engaging with community-based researchers on long-term projects that could support strengthening and sustaining their communities.[21]

TOWARD THE FUTURE WITH SPORT JUSTICE

Within the last decade, the Black Lives Matter movement has been the catalyst for athletes, several grassroots organizations, everyday citizens, and society at large to take action on tangible societal change. As mentioned in chapters 3 and 4, Black athletes and their allies have paved the way on illuminating several social issues such as police brutality, mental health, workplace equity, and public policy. While sport and politics continue to dominate the global conversation, the individual perspectives within this chapter show that there is still much work to be done for tangible social change. However, athletes are no longer sitting on the proverbial sidelines while social injustice runs rampant within our global society. They have become more educated on matters such as diversity, equity, inclusion, education, police brutality, socioeconomic development, and overall human rights. The SJM is here to stay.

For example, in his continued effort to combat social injustice, Colin Kaepernick launched the Autopsy Initiative through his Know Your Rights Camp nonprofit organization. Through this platform,

> the Autopsy Initiative will collaborate with board-certified forensic pathologists who perform autopsies and will disclose their preliminary findings, as well as issue final reports to the families.[22]

Since the revitalization of athlete activism over the last few years, several sport-specific social justice organizations have formed. One in particular is Black Players for Change (BPC). Formed in 2020, BPC is an organization featuring over 170+ soccer players, coaches, and staff members associated with Major League Soccer (MLS), the highest level of men's professional soccer in the United States. The organization was formed to help eradicate inequality in society. More so, their focus is on human rights issues, policy reform, and partnerships in the movement for a just society.

In conjunction with MLS leadership, BPC and others focused on racial equality provided the necessary input to MLS's Diversity, Equity, and Inclusion Committee to update their policies. Similar to the Rooney Rule, MLS has updated their policies to include the following:

- A requirement to ensure that the finalist pool for an open sporting position includes two or more nonwhite candidates, one of whom must be Black or African American, as part of a renewed effort to prioritize opportunities for Black candidates. Previously, the policy only required one diverse candidate to be interviewed for an open position.

- A new requirement to demonstrate an equal interview process and comparable interview experience for all candidates in the finalist pool for an open sporting position.
- Clarification of public sanctions for teams that fail to abide by the policy, including up to $50,000 fines for first offenses, up to $100,000 fines for second offenses, and fines of more than $100,000 (under the commissioner's discretion) for third offenses and beyond. Previously, the commissioner had sole discretion to impose sanctions as he saw fit.
- A new commitment to review the policy annually and update it as needed.
- The addition of a definition of "underrepresented groups" to specify that this term includes Black or African American, Hispanic/Latino(a), American Indian/Alaska Native, Asian, Hawaiian/Pacific Islander, Canadian Indigenous, Canadian First Nations, women, and members of the LGBTQ+ community.
- The addition of a specific list of first-team sporting positions and academy sporting positions to which this policy applies.
- The creation of a Diversity Policy Portal (DPP) in which clubs must submit all details of vacant sporting positions and include information related to all candidates in the final candidate pool.
- The addition of specific guidelines for a process to request waivers to the policy, granted only in extenuating circumstances.[23]

In 2016, several high-profile members of the women's national soccer team (USWNT) filed a federal equal-pay complaint against U.S. Soccer, which serves as the governing body of soccer in the United States. The lawsuit claimed that female soccer players were being paid significantly less than their male counterparts. The next few years saw a battle between the players and U.S. Soccer as the parties could not agree to terms.

In 2022, the USWNT's cased gained progress when they and U.S. Soccer agreed to a settlement in which the governing body would pay $22 million in back pay to the players. Additionally, the governing body will place $2 million into a fund that supports USWNT retirement goals and charitable organizations. In a joint statement released by USWNT and U.S. Soccer, they said, "We are pleased to announce that, contingent on the negotiations of a new collective bargaining agreement, we will have resolved our longstanding dispute over equal pay and proudly stand together in a shared commitment to advancing equality in soccer."[24]

This book has discussed how sport and politics have played an instrumental role in changing society for the better. From Garvey to the Black Panther Party to social movements such as Black Lives Matter catalyzing renewed activism, progress has been made for social justice. The future of sport should be one in which Black coaches receive fair opportunities to lead college and professional sports franchises. It should also be one where sports organizations continue to progress toward positive police and community relations. It should be one where athletes have the freedom to challenge lawmakers to make sweeping changes that are not only introduced as legislation but are made into law. Although athletes have been told to "shut up and dribble," they have learned to ignore those cues in the pursuance of true societal change. They are becoming educated on the issues that need policy reform. They will need support from lawmakers, grassroots organizers, scholars, and other leaders. Now is not the time to stick to sports. Rather, it is a time to recognize sport as a legitimate power to create substantial social change.

Bibliography

Abusaid, Shaddi. "Muhammad Ali's Return to the Ring Electrified Atlanta, Black Community." *Atlanta Journal-Constitution*, February 24, 2020. https://www.ajc .com/lifestyles/muhammad-ali-return-the-ring-electrified-atlanta-black-community /S22y8j0zLW7K4iGSPuOD8H.

Adams, John S. "Toward an Understanding of Inequity." *Journal of Abnormal and Social Psychology* 67, no. 5 (1963): 422–36. https://doi.org/10.1037/h0040968.

Adande, J. A. "Purpose of I Can't Breathe T-Shirts." ESPN, December 10, 2014. https://www.espn.com/nba/story/_/id/12010612/nba-stars-making-statement -wearing-breathe-shirts.

Ajom, Jacob. "IWD 2021: NBA, BAL Launch Gender Equality Initiative in Africa." *Vanguard*, March 12, 2021. https://www.vanguardngr.com/2021/03/iwd-2021-nba -bal-launch-gender-equality-initiative-in-africa.

Alitvavoli, Rayeheh, and Ehsan Kaveh. "The U.S. Media's Effect on Public's Crime Expectations: A Cycle of Cultivation and Agenda-Setting Theory." *Societies* 8, no. 58 (Summer 2018): 2–9. https://doi:10.3390/soc8030058.

Allen, Lisa. "Faculty Spotlight: Joseph N. Cooper." *UMass Boston News*, January 15, 2021. https://www.umb.edu/news/detail/faculty_spotlight_joseph_n_cooper.

Allport, Gordon W. *The Nature of Prejudice*. Boston: Addison-Wesley, 1954.

Alvarez, Lizette, and Cara Buckley. "Zimmerman Is Acquitted in Trayvon Martin Killing." *New York Times*, July 13, 2013. https://www.nytimes.com/2013/07/14/us /george-zimmerman-verdict-trayvon-martin.html.

Ames, Annabel. "Abigail Hollis Found Frustration and Inspiration as Member of Concerned Student 1950." *Vox*, November 16, 2017. https://www.voxmagazine .com/magazine/abigail-hollis-found-frustration-and-inspiration-as-member-of -concerned-student-1950/article_fe38fc6c-ca42-11e7-980b-e3c2806fcc6a.html.

Anderson, Monica. "The Hashtag #BlackLivesMatter Emerges: Social Activism on Twitter." Pew Research Center: Internet & Technology, August 15, 2016. https://www.pewresearch.org/internet/2016/08/15/the-hashtag-blacklivesmatter -emerges-social-activism-on-twitter.

Andre, Claire, and Manuel Velasquez. "The Just World Theory." *Issues in Ethics* (Markkula Center for Applied Ethics) 3, no. 2 (Spring 1990).

Arkin, William, Tracy Connor, and Jim Miklaszewski. "Dallas Shooter Micah Johnson Was Army Veteran and 'Loner.'" NBC News, July 8, 2016. https://www.nbcnews.com/storyline/dallas-police-ambush/dallas-shooter-micah-xavier-johnson-was-army-veteran-n606101.

"Arthur Ashe." Biography, accessed November 13, 2021. https://www.biography.com/athlete/arthur-ashe.

Aschburner, Steve. "Coronavirus Pandemic Causes NBA to Suspend Season after Player Tests Positive." NBA.com, March 12, 2020. https://www.nba.com/news/coronavirus-pandemic-causes-nba-suspend-season.

Ault, Alicia. "Althea Gibson's Momentous Achievement." *Smithsonian Magazine*, June 1, 2021. https://www.smithsonianmag.com/smithsonian-institution/sixty-five-years-ago-althea-gibson-broke-color-line-french-open-180977859.

Bae, Gawon, and Jill Martin. "International Olympic Committee Suspends Its Action on Raven Saunders' Podium Protest after Her Mother's Death." CNN, updated August 4, 2021. https://www.cnn.com/2021/08/04/sport/olympian-raven-saunders-protest-action-suspended/index.html.

Bates, Karen Grisby. "In 1968, Arthur Ashe Made History at the US Open." NPR, September 10, 2018. https://www.npr.org/sections/codeswitch/2018/09/10/646213901/in-1968-arthur-ashe-made-history-at-the-u-s-open.

Berkowitz, Steve. "Proposed California Bill Could Create New Pressure in NCAA Name, Image, and Likeness Debate." *USA Today*, updated December 8, 2020. https://www.usatoday.com/story/sports/college/2020/12/07/ncaa-could-face-pressure-new-california-name-image-likeness-bill/3856850001.

Bierman, Noah, W. J. Hennigan, and Joseph Tanfani. "Baltimore Racked by Violence; Governor Calls Out National Guard." *Los Angeles Times*, April 27, 2015. https://www.latimes.com/nation/la-na-freddie-gray-funeral-baltimore-20150427-story.html.

Bies, Robert J. "International (In)justice: The Sacred and the Profane." In *Advances in Organizational Justice*, edited by Jerald Greenberg and Russell Cropanzano, 89–118. Stanford University Press, 2001.

Blankstein, Andrew, and Danielle Silva. "LeBron James' Los Angeles Home Vandalized with 'N-Word' Graffiti." NBC News, updated June 1, 2017. https://www.nbcnews.com/news/us-news/lebron-james-los-angeles-home-vandalized-n-word-graffiti-n766651.

Bomboy, Scott. "The Supreme Court Decision That Saved Muhammad Ali's Boxing Career." *Constitution Daily*, June 4, 2016. https://constitutioncenter.org/blog/alie28099s-supreme-court-decision-was-biggest-victory.

Bond, Paul. "Study: TV Violence Linked to 'Mean World Syndrome.'" *Hollywood Reporter*, June 18, 2014. https://www.hollywoodreporter.com/news/general-news/study-tv-violence-linked-mean-712890.

Bonk, Thomas. "Late Jurist, Sifford Helped to Diversify the Game." *LA Times*, June 28, 2001. https://www.latimes.com/archives/la-xpm-2001-jun-28-sp-15978-story.html.

Booker, Brakkton. "Democrats Push 'Abolition Amendment' to Fully Erase Slavery from U.S. Constitution." NPR, December 3, 2020. https://www.npr .org/2020/12/03/942413221/democrats-push-abolition-amendment-to-fully-erase -slavery-from-u-s-constitution.

Boren, Cindy. "Arian Foster and Three Dolphins Teammates Protest during National Anthem Protest." *Washington Post*, September 11, 2016. https://www .washingtonpost.com/news/early-lead/wp/2016/09/11/arian-foster-and-three -dolphins-teammates-protest-during-national-anthem.

Borger, Julian. "Insurrection Day: When White Supremacist Terror Came to the US Capitol." *Guardian*, January 9, 2021. https://www.theguardian.com/us-news/2021 /jan/09/us-capitol-insurrection-white-supremacist-terror.

Boyer, Nate. "An Open Letter to Colin Kaepernick, from a Green Beret-Turned -Long Snapper." *Army Times*, August 30, 2016. https://www.armytimes.com/opin- ion/2016/08/30/an-open-letter-to-colin-kaepernick-from-a-green-beret-turned-long -snapper.

Brandt, Andrew. "Business of Football: The Supreme Court Sends a Message to the NCAA." *Sports Illustrated*, June 29, 2021. https://www.si.com/nfl/2021/06/29 /business-of-football-supreme-court-unanimous-ruling.

Breech, John. "Browns Refuse Apology to Cleveland Cops over Andrew Hawkins' Actions." CBS Sports, December 15, 2014. https://www.cbssports.com/nfl/news /browns-refuse-apology-to-cleveland-cops-over-andrew-hawkins-actions.

———. "Colin Kaepernick, Eric Reid Collusion Settlement: Duo Reportedly Split Less than $10 Million." CBS Sports, March 21, 2019. https://www.cbssports.com /nfl/news/colin-kaepernick-eric-reid-collusion-settlement-duo-reportedly-split -less-than-10-million.

———. "Here Are the 11 Players Who Joined Colin Kaepernick's Protest in Week 1." CBS Sports, September 12, 2016. https://www.cbssports.com/nfl/news/here-are -the-11-players-who-joined-colin-kaepernicks-protest-in-week-1.

———. "Roger Goodell Calls Out Donald Trump for Making 'Divisive Comments' about the NFL." CBS Sports, September 23, 2017. https://www.cbssports.com/nfl /news/roger-goodell-calls-out-donald-trump-for-making-divisive-comments-about -the-nfl.

Breer, Albert. "How NFL Teams Are Managing the Transition for This Year's Rookie Class." *Sports Illustrated*, June 25, 2020. https://www.si.com/nfl/2020/06/25/nfl -los-angeles-rams-rookie-transition.

Breuninger, Kevin. "Biden Signs Juneteenth Bill, Creating New Federal Holiday Commemorating End of Slavery in U.S." CNBC, June 17, 2021. https://www.cnbc .com/2021/06/17/juneteenth-federal-holiday-biden-signs-bill.html.

Brinson, Will. "The 49ers Would've Cut Colin Kaepernick If He Hadn't Opted Out of His Contract." CBS Sports, May 31, 2017. https://www.cbssports.com/nfl/news /the-49ers-wouldve-cut-colin-kaepernick-if-he-hadnt-opted-out-of-his-contract.

Bromwich, Jonah Engel. "Michael Jordan Says He Is 'Deeply Troubled' by Recent Police-Related Violence." *New York Times*, July 25, 2016. https://www.nytimes. com/2016/07/26/sports/basketball/michael-jordan-statement-on-police-related -violence.html.

Brooks, Scott N., and Dexter Blackman. "Introduction: African Americans and the History of Sport-New Perspectives." *Journal of African American History* 96, no. 4 (2011): 441–47.

Brownstein, Ronald. "The Rage Unifying Boomers and Gen Z." *Atlantic*, June 18, 2020. https://www.theatlantic.com/politics/archive/2020/06/todays-protest-movements-are-as-big-as-the-1960s/613207.

Burgos, Carlos, Victoria Alvarez, and Myfanwy Taylor. "We're Fighting to Show What Urban Development for People, Not Profit, Can Look Like." *Guardian*, August 11, 2021. https://www.theguardian.com/commentisfree/2021/aug/11/urban-development-for-people-not-for-profit-north-london-latin-village.

Cannizzaro, Mark. "Charlie Sifford, the Jackie Robinson of Golf, Dead at 92." *New York Post*, February 4, 2015. https://nypost.com/2015/02/04/charlie-sifford-the-jackie-robinson-of-golf-dead-at-92.

Carey, Meaghan, Daniel S. Mason, and Laura Misener. "Social Responsibility and the Competitive Bid Process for Major Sporting Events." *Journal of Sport and Social Issues* 35, no. 3 (2011): 246–63. https://doi.org/10.1177/0193723511416985.

Chan, Melissa. "What to Know about Alton Sterling's Police Shooting Death in Baton Rouge." *Time*, July 6, 2016. https://time.com/4395459/alton-sterling-baton-rouge-police-shooting.

Christian, Mark. "Marcus Garvey and African Unity: Lessons for the Future from the Past." *Journal of Black Studies* 39, no. 2 (2008): 316–31.

Cillizza, Chris. "Donald Trump's Allies Are Going to Make America Great Again. Again. Seriously." CNN, October 5, 2021. https://www.cnn.com/2021/10/05/politics/donald-trump-super-pac/index.html.

Clayton, Andy. "Santa Clara's Top Cop Vows to 'Provide Safe Environment at Levi's Stadium' despite Colin Kaepernick's 'Hurtful' Comments against Police." *New York Daily News*, September 3, 2016. https://www.nydailynews.com/sports/football/threat-levi-stadium-safe-police-chief-article-1.2777134.

Colquitt, Jason A., Donald E. Conlon, Michael J. Wesson, Christopher O. L. H. Porter, and K. Yee Ng. "Justice at the Millennium: A Meta-Analytic Review of 25 Years of Organizational Justice Research." *Journal of Applied Psychology* 86, no. 3 (2001): 425–45. https://doi.org/10.1037/0021-9010.86.3.425.

Conway, Tyler. "NBA Foundation Announce $3M+ in Grants to Support Black Economic Empowerment." *Bleacher Report*, April 5, 2021. https://bleacherreport.com/articles/2939352-nba-foundation-announce-3m-in-grants-to-support-black-economic-empowerment.

Cooper, Joseph N., Charles Macaulay, and Saturnino H Rodriguez. "Race and Resistance: A Typology of African American Sport Activism." *International Review for the Sociology of Sport* 54, no. 2 (2019): 151–81.

Cottle, Rex L. "Economics of the Professional Golfers' Association Tour." *Social Science Quarterly* 62, no. 4 (1981): 721.

Cucinotta, Domenico, and Maurizio Vanelli. "WHO Declares COVID-19 a Pandemic." *Acta Biomed* 91, no. 1 (March 2020): 157–60. https//doi.org/10.23750/abm.v91i1.9397.

Cunningham, George B., and Michael R. Regan Jr. "Political Activism, Racial Identity and the Commercial Endorsement of Athletes." *International Review for the Sociology of Sport* 47, no. 6 (2012): 657–69. https://doi.org/10.1177/1012690211416358.

Daniels, Tim. "Report: NFL, Players Coalition Finalize $90M Social Justice Partnership." *Bleacher Report*, May 22, 2018. https://bleacherreport.com/articles/2777275-report-nfl-players-coalition-finalize-90m-social-justice-partnership.

Dator, James. "Maya Moore Is Now Married to Jonathan Irons, the Man She Helped Free from Prison." SBNation.com, September 16, 2020. https://www.sbnation.com/wnba/2020/9/16/21439514/maya-moore-married-jonathan-irons-wnba.

Day, Elizabeth. "#BlackLivesMatter: The Birth of a New Civil Rights Movement." *Guardian*, July 19, 2015. https://www.theguardian.com/world/2015/jul/19/blacklivesmatter-birth-civil-rights-movement.

Decourcy, Mike. "If NCAA Had Never Taken on Ed O'Bannon, It Might Not Have Been Dunked on So Furiously by the Supreme Court." *Sporting News*, accessed June 21, 2021. https://www.sportingnews.com/us/ncaa-basketball/news/if-ncaa-had-never-taken-on-ed-obannon-it-might-not-have-been-dunked-on-so-ferociously-by-the-supreme-court/s01kygckfegc14658trnip7k2.

Deetz, Stanley. *Democracy in an Age of Corporate Colonization.* Albany, NY: SUNY Press, 1992.

Deitsch, Richard. "Why the NFL's Ratings Saw a Steep Decline in 2017." *Sports Illustrated*, January 3, 2018. https://www.si.com/media/2018/01/03/nfl-ratings-decline-espn-fox-nbc-network-tv.

Deliso, Meridith. "Timeline: The Impact of George Floyd's Death in Minneapolis and Beyond." ABC News, April 21, 2021. https://abcnews.go.com/US/timeline-impact-george-floyds-death-minneapolis/story?id=70999322.

Dirlam, Zach. "There's No Crying in College: The Case against Paying College Athletes." *Bleacher Report*, April, 2, 2013. https://bleacherreport.com/articles/1588301-theres-no-crying-in-college-the-case-against-paying-college-athletes.

Dreier, Peter. "The Man behind the March: Remembering Bayard Rustin." *Commonwealth Magazine*, May 21, 2012. https://www.commonwealmagazine.org/man-behind-march.

Dukes, Kristine Nicole, and Sarah E. Gaither. "Black Racial Stereotypes and Victim Blaming: Implications for Media Coverage and Criminal Proceedings in Cases of Police Violence against Racial and Ethnic Minorities." *Journal of Social Issues* 73, no. 4 (2017): 789–807. https://doi.org/10.1111.josi.12248.

Dutton, Sarah, Jennifer De Pinto, Anthony Salvanto, and Fred Baukus. "Have the Goals of the Civil Rights Movement Have Been Achieved?" CBS News, March 4, 2015. https://www.cbsnews.com/news/have-the-goals-of-the-civil-rights-movement-have-been-achieved.

Edelman, Marc. "Explaining Eric Reid's Collusion Grievance against the NFL." *Forbes*, May 3, 2018. https://www.forbes.com/sites/marcedelman/2018/05/03/explaining-eric-reids-collusion-grievance-against-the-nfl.

Eig, Jonathan. "The Cleveland Summit and Muhammad Ali: The True Story." *The Undefeated*, June 1, 2017. https://theundefeated.com/features/the-cleveland -summit-muhammad-ali.

Eisenberg, Jeff. "Iconic Sports Commercials: Charles Barkley's 'I Am Not a Role Model.'" *Yahoo!*, July 16, 2019. https://www.yahoo.com/now/iconic-sports -commercials-charles-barkleys-i-am-not-a-role-model-055726035.html.

El-Nawawy, Mohammed, and Mohamad Hamas Elmasry. "Valuing Victims: A Comparative Framing Analysis of *The Washington Post*'s Coverage of Violent Attacks against Muslims and Non-Muslims." *International Journal of Communication* 11 (2017).

Elfman, Lois. "Black Male Student-Athletes Still Face Harsh Inequities." Diverse Education, March 11, 2018. https://www.diverseeducation.com/home /article/15102161/black-male-student-athletes-still-face-harsh-inequities.

Euchner, Jim. "The Medium Is the Message." *Research-Technology Management* 59, no. 5 (2016): 9–11. https://doi.org/10.1080/08956308.2016.1209068.

Farrell, Jenny. "Paul Robeson: Activist, Communist, and Spokesperson for the Oppressed of the Earth." *Culture Matters*, March 31, 2018. https://www.cul-turematters.org.uk/index.php/arts/music/item/2772-paul-robeson-activist-and -spokesperson-for-the-oppressed.

Florio, Mike. "St. Louis Police Officers Association Condemns Rams' Ferguson Gesture." *Pro Football Talk*, November 30, 2014. https://profootballtalk.nbcsports .com/2014/11/30/st-louis-police-officers-association-condemns-rams-ferguson -gesture.

Folley, Aris. "LeBron James Responds to Criticism: 'I Would Never Shut Up about Things That Are Wrong.'" *The Hill*, February 28, 2021. https://thehill .com/blogs/in-the-know/in-the-know/540872-lebron-james-responds-to-criticism -i-would-never-shut-up-about.

Foran, Clare. "A Year of Black Lives Matter." *Atlantic*, December 31, 2015. https://www.theatlantic.com/politics/archive/2015/12/black-lives-matter/421839.

Forstater, Mathew. "From Civil Rights to Economic Security: Bayard Rustin and the African American Struggle for Full Employment, 1945–1978." *International Journal of Political Economy* 36, no. 3 (2007): 63–74.

Francois, Myriam. "Adam Traore: How George Floyd's Death Energized French Protests." BBC News, May 19, 2021. https://www.bbc.com/news/world-us-can ada-57176500.

Franklin, Jonathan. "Louisville Police Officer Who Fatally Shot Breonna Taylor Appeals to Get His Job Back." NPR, November 10, 2021. https://www.npr .org/2021/11/10/1054042088/louisville-police-officer-breonna-taylor-appeals-job.

Fredrickson, Dave. "The NFL's Reversal on 'Race Norming' Reveals How Pervasive Medical Racism Remains." NBC News, June 8, 2021. https://www.nbcnews.com /think/opinion/nfl-s-reversal-race-norming-reveals-how-pervasive-medical -racism-ncna1269992.

Frey, James H., and D. Stanley Eitzen. "Sport and Society." *Annual Review of Sociology* 17 (1991): 503–22.

Gallagher, J. J. "US Soccer Star Joins Kaepernick in National Anthem Protest." ABC News, September 4, 2016. https://abcnews.go.com/US/us-soccer-star-joins -kaepernick-kneeling-protest-national/story?id=41866258.

Gatto, Tom. "Police, Rams Can't Agree on Definition of 'Apology.'" *Sporting News*, January 12, 2014. https://www.sportingnews.com/au/nfl/news/hands-up-don-t -shoot-st-louis-rams-ferguson-protests-kevin-demoff-apology-st-louis-police -slpoa/kgjkcjkh0sfz16mvtqiqz4qrv.

Gardell, Mattias. *In the Name of Elijah Muhammad: Louis Farrakhan and the Nation of Islam*. Durham, NC: Duke University Press, 1996.

Gay, Jason. "Muhammad Ali Shook Up the World." *Wall Street Journal*, updated June 4, 2016. https://www.wsj.com/articles/muhammad-ali-shook-up-the -world-1465022480.

Gentile, Sean. "The Steelers' Political Machine and the PAC Supporting Pittsburgh Candidates." The Athletic, October 29, 2020. https://theathletic .com/2167116/2020/10/29/pittsburgh-steelers-pac-nfl-political-donations.

Geva, Dorit. "Selective Service, the Gender-Ordered Family, and the Rational Informality of the American State." *American Journal of Sociology* 121, no. 1 (2015): 171–204.

Gill, Emmitt L., Jr. "Hands Up, Don't Shoot or Shut Up and Play Ball? Fan-Generated Media Views of the Ferguson Five." *Journal of Human Behavior in the Social Environment* 26, nos. 3–4 (2016): 400–412. https://doi.org/10.1080/10911359.20 16.1139990.

Given, Karen. "Walter Byers: The Man Who Built the NCAA, then Tried to Tear It Down." WBUR, October 13, 2017. https://www.wbur.org/onlyagame/2017/10/13 /walter-byers-ncaa.

Gold, Jonathan. "Browder v. Gayle: The Most Important Civil Rights Case You've Never Heard Of." *Learning for Justice*, Summer 2016. https://www.learningfor justice.org/magazine/summer-2016/browder-v-gayle.

Goldberg, Rob. "Colin Kaepernick's Know Your Rights Camp Gives $1.75 for COVID, Social Causes." *Bleacher Report*, July 15, 2020. https://bleacherre-port.com/articles/2900286-colin-kaepernicks-know-your-rights-camp-gives-175m -for-covid-social-causes.

Gray, Frances Clayton, and Yanick Lamb. *Born to Win: The Authorized Biography of Althea Gibson*. Hoboken, NJ: Wiley, 2004.

Guardian Sport. "Senator Loeffler Objects to WNBA's Black Lives Matter Tie-in 'Removal of Jesus.'" *Guardian*, July 7, 2020. https://www.theguardian.com /sport/2020/jul/07/kelly-loeffler-black-lives-matter-wnba-atlanta-dream.

Hagemann, Hannah, and Lynsey Jeffery. "George Floyd Reverberates Globally; Thousands Protest in Germany, U.K., New Zealand." NPR, May 31, 2020. https://www.npr.org/2020/05/31/866428272/george-floyd-reverberates-globally -thousands-protest-in-germany-u-k-canada.

Haines, Matt. "Effects of Jim Crow Era Live on in Modern America, Some Say." VOA News, April 22, 2021. https://www.voanews.com/a/usa_effects-jim-crow -era-live-modern-america-some-say/6204908.html.

Haislop, Tadd. "What Is the NFL's National Anthem Protest Policy? Here Are the Rules for Kneeling in 2020." *Sporting News*, September 20, 2020. https://www.sportingnews.com/us/nfl/news/nfl-national-anthem-policy-2020-kneeling-protests/1o88fwivdxvqu1d8nnbiw5dw3z.

Hanson, Hilary, and Simon McCormack. "Fox News Suggests Black Lives Matter Is a 'Murder' Movement, 'Hate Group.'" *HuffPost*, updated September 1, 2015. https://www.huffpost.com/entry/black-lives-matter-fox-news-hate-group_n_55e5c102e4b0b7a9633a3b12.

Harig, Bob. "Masters Chairman Fred Ridley against Boycott over Georgia Voting Law." ESPN, April 7, 2021. https://www.espn.com/golf/story/_/id/31210086/masters-chairman-fred-ridley-burdening-augusta-boycott-georgia-voting-law.

Herb, Jeremy, Manu Raju, and Lauren Fox. "Democrats Unveil Two Articles of Impeachment against Trump." CNN, December 10, 2019. https://www.cnn.com/2019/12/10/politics/impeachment-articles-announced/index.html.

Herring, Chris. "Carmelo Anthony Marches with Protesters in Baltimore." *Wall Street Journal*, April 30, 2015. https://www.wsj.com/articles/carmelo-anthony-marches-with-protesters-in-baltimore-1430440077.

Hill, Jemele. "The Heat's Hoodies as Change Agent." ESPN, March 26, 2012. https://www.espn.com/espn/commentary/story/_/page/hill-120326/lebron-james-other-athletes-protest-trayvon-martin-shooting-show-change-agent-power-sports.

Holmes, Brian. "Before Signing Jackie Robinson to the Dodgers, Branch Rickey Was a Failed Boise Lawyer." KTVB.com, April 15, 2021. https://www.ktvb.com/article/news/local/208/how-failed-boise-lawyer-helped-jackie-robinson-integrate-the-mlb/277-c72db0f7-ca68-4675-b1b6-0e93e5a269ef.

"Houston Texans Owner Bob McNair Apologies for Remark." NFL.com, October 27, 2017. https://www.nfl.com/news/houston-texans-owner-bob-mcnair-apologizes-for-remark-0ap3000000868160.

IE Staff. "Colin Kaepernick's New Initiative Will Offer Free Autopsies for Those Killed in Police-Related Incidents." *Inside Edition*, February 24, 2022. https://www.insideedition.com/colin-kaepernicks-new-initiative-will-offer-free-autopsies-for-those-killed-in-police-related-73447.

Imani, Zellie. "Everything You Need to Know about the Students' Demands ahead of #StudentBlackOut National Day of Action." *Atlanta Black Star*, November 18, 2015. https://atlantablackstar.com/2015/11/18/everything-you-need-to-know-about-the-students-demands-ahead-of-studentblackout-national-day-of-action.

"It's Time for a Racial Reckoning in College Sports: Knight Commission Releases Plan to Create Racial Equity for Black College Athletes." Knight Commission, May 12, 2021. https://www.knightcommission.org/2021/05/racial-equity.

Jackson, Wilton. "Zlatan Ibrahimovic: LeBron James, Other Athletes Should 'Do What You're Good At,' Stay Out of Politics." *Sports Illustrated*, February 26, 2021. https://www.si.com/soccer/2021/02/26/zlatan-ibrahimovic-lebron-james-lakers-athlete-activism-politics.

Janken, Kenneth R. "African American and Francophone Black Intellectuals during the Harlem Renaissance." *The Historian* 60, no. 3 (1998): 487–505.

Jervis, Rick. "Black Americans Got the Right to Vote 150 Years Ago, but Voter Suppression Still a Problem." *USA Today*, February 3, 2020. https://www.usatoday .com/story/news/nation/2020/02/03/black-voting-rights-15th-amendment-still| -challenged-after-150-years/4587160002.

Kaiser, Cheryl R., and Jennifer S. Pratt-Hyatt. "Distributing Prejudice Unequally: Do Whites Direct Their Prejudice toward Strongly Identified Minorities?" *Journal of Personality and Social Psychology* 96, no. 2 (2009): 432–45. https://doi.org/10.1037/a0012877.

Kalman-Lamb, Nathan, Derek Silva, and Johanna Mellis. "I Signed My Life to Rich White Guys: Athletes on the Racial Dynamics of College Sports." *Guardian*, March 17, 2021. https://www.theguardian.com/sport/2021/mar/17/college-sports -racial-dynamics.

Kaplan, Hasan. "Belief in a Just World, Religiosity and Victim Blaming." *Archive for the Psychology of Religion* 34, no. 3 (2012): 397–409. https://doi .org/10.1163/15736121-12341246.

Kaste, Martin. "More than 17,000 Deaths Caused by Police Have Been Misclassified since 1980." NPR, October 1, 2021. https://www.npr.org/2021/10/01/1041989880 /deaths-caused-by-police-misclassified.

Katella, Kathy. "Our Pandemic Year—A COVID-19 Timeline." *Yale Medicine*, March 9, 2021. https://www.yalemedicine.org/news/covid-timeline.

Katkov, Mark. "Noose Left in Black NASCAR Driver Bubba Wallace's Garage Stall at Racetrack." NPR, June 22, 2020. https://www.npr.org/sections/live -updates-protests-for-racial-justice/2020/06/22/881539780/noose-left-in-black -drivers-garage-stall-at-nascar-race-track.

Katz, Brigit. "Althea Gibson, Who Smashed through Racial Barriers in Tennis, Honored with Statue at U.S. Open." *Smithsonian Magazine*, August 28, 2019. https://www.smithsonianmag.com/smart-news/althea-gibson-who-smashed -through-racial-barriers-tennis-honored-statue-us-open-180973001.

Kilgo, Danielle, and Rache R. Mourao. "Media Effects and Marginalized Ideas: Relationships among Media Consumption and Support for Black Lives Matter." *International Journal of Communication* 13 (2019): 4287–305.

King, Gilbert. "What Paul Robeson Said." *Smithsonian*, September 13, 2011. https://www.smithsonianmag.com/history/what-paul-robeson-said-77742433.

Knoblauch, Austin. "NFL Owners Approve National Anthem Policy for 2018." NFL. com, May 23, 2018. https://www.nfl.com/news/nfl-owners-approve-national-anthem -policy-for-2018-0ap3000000933971.

Knopper, Steve. "The True Story of N.W.A. Playing 'Fuck the Police' Live in Detroit." *GQ*, July 21, 2020. https://www.gq.com/story/nwa-fuck-the-police-live-detroit.

"Know Your Rights Camp 10 Points." Know Your Rights Camp, accessed November 30, 2021. https://www.knowyourrightscamp.com/who-we-are.

Lamb, Chris. "The First Trip to Spring Training: A Jackie Robinson Story You May Not Know from 75 Years Ago." *USA Today*, February 17, 2021. https://www.usatoday.com/story/sports/2021/02/17/jackie-robinson-spring-training -story-75-years-ago/4488581001.

———. "When a Black Boxing Champion Beat the 'Great White Hope,' All Hell Broke Loose." *The Conversation*, June 30, 2021. https://theconversation .com/when-a-black-boxing-champion-beat-the-great-white-hope-all-hell-broke -loose-163413.

Langley, Jabez Ayodele. "Garveyism and African Nationalism." *Race & Class* 11, no. 2 (1969): 157–72.

Lardieri, Alexa. "Trump to Hannity: You Can't Disrespect Our Flag." *U.S. News*, October 12, 2017. https://www.usnews.com/news/politics/articles/2017-10-12 /trump-to-hannity-you-cant-disrespect-our-flag.

Laughland, Oliver. "*Plessy v Ferguson* Upheld Segregation—Now Plessy's Family Seeks a Pardon." *Guardian*, November 12, 2021. https://www.theguardian.com /us-news/2021/nov/12/plessy-ferguson-jim-crow-segregation-pardon-new-orleans.

Laughland, Oliver, and Jon Swaine. "Six Baltimore Officers Suspended over Police -Van Death of Freddie Gray." *Guardian*, April 20, 2015. https://www.theguardian. com/us-news/2015/apr/20/baltimore-officers-suspended-death-freddie-gray.

Lawrence, Andrew "Trump Wanted to 'Kaepernick' Bubba Wallace. Instead, He Made Him Too Big to Fail." *Guardian*, July 7, 2020. https://www.theguardian.com /sport/2020/jul/07/bubba-wallace-donald-trump-twitter-nascar.

Lemke, Wilfred. "The Role of Sport in Achieving the Sustainable Development Goals." United Nations, accessed November 1, 2021. https://www.un.org/en /chronicle/article/role-sport-achieving-sustainable-development-goals.

Lerner, Melvin J. *The Belief in a Just World: A Fundamental Delusion*. Boston: Springer, 1980.

Liu, Yvonne. "Disconnected Youth in Los Angeles." Advancement Project CA, March 28, 2018. https://www.advancementprojectca.org/blog/disconnected-youth-in-los-angeles.

Lopez, German. "Sandra Bland's Death Was a Suicide. That Doesn't Let the Justice System off the Hook." *Vox*, July 14, 2016. https://www.vox.com/2016/7/14/12185324 /sandra-bland-suicide-jail.

Lozano, Alicia Victoria, and David K. Li. "Super Bowl Host Inglewood, California, Is Transforming on Multiple Fronts." NBC News, updated February 13, 2022. https://www.nbcnews.com/business/inglewood-demographic-changes-facts-dive rsity-rcna8227.

Macri, Kenneth J. "Not Just a Game: Sport and Society in the United States." *Inquiries* 4, no. 8 (2012): 1. http://www.inquiriesjournal.com/articles/1664/not-just-a -game-sport-and-society-in-the-united-states.

Madani, Doha. "Colin Kaepernick Attending Private Workout for NFL Teams." NBC News, November 12, 2019. https://www.nbcnews.com/news/sports /colin-kaepernick-attending-private-workout-nfl-teams-n1081026.

Majeed, Arshad. "LA Clippers, Aspiration Sign $300-Million-Plus Arena Sponsor Deal." *Verve Times*, September 27, 2021. https://vervetimes.com/la-clippers -aspiration-sign-300-million-plus-arena-sponsor-deal.

Maranzani, Barbara. "Martin Luther King Jr. and Malcolm X Only Met Once." Biography, January 19, 2021. https://www.biography.com/news/martin-luther-king -jr-malcolm-x-meeting.

Margolin, Emma. "Make America Great Again—Who Said It First?" NBC News, September 9, 2016. https://www.nbcnews.com/politics/2016-election/make -america-great-again-who-said-it-first-n645716.

Masur, Louise P. "How the Emancipation Proclamation Came to Be Signed." *Smithsonian Magazine*, January 2013. https://www.smithsonianmag.com/history/how -the-emancipation-proclamation-came-to-be-signed-165533991.

Maxouris, Christina. "Kyle Rittenhouse Was Acquitted on All Charges. Here's What We Know about the 3 Men Shot." CNN, November 19, 2021. https://www.cnn .com/2021/11/01/us/kyle-rittenhouse-shooting-victims-trial/index.html.

Maya, Adam. "Anquan Boldin on NFL's Social Justice Initiatives: 'What Is Happening Now Was the Vision' of Players Coalition." NFL.com, September 15, 2020. https://www.nfl.com/news/anquan-boldin-on-nfl-s-social-justice-initiatives-what -is-happening-now-was-the-.

McBride, Colin. "The Kansas City Monarchs (1920–1965)." BlackPast.org, March 28, 2014. https://www.blackpast.org/african-american-history/kansas-city -monarchs-1920-1965.

McCann, Michael. "Why the NCAA Lost Its Latest Landmark Case in the Battle over What Schools Can Offer Athletes." *Sports Illustrated*, March 8, 2019. https://www .si.com/college/2019/03/09/ncaa-antitrust-lawsuit-claudia-wilken-alston-jenkins.

McCarriston, Shanna. "Bubba Wallace' Black Lives Matter Scheme Car from Martinsville Race Can Now Be Ordered Online." CBS Sports, June 18, 2020. https://www.cbssports.com/nascar/news/bubba-wallace-black-lives-matter -scheme-car-from-martinsville-race-can-now-be-ordered-online.

McManamon, Pat. "Police Decry Andrew Hawkins Protest." ESPN, December 14, 2014. https://www.espn.com/nfl/story/_/id/12030748/andrew-hawkins-cleveland -browns-wears-protest-shirt-police-seek-apology.

Medina, Mark. "How NBA Teams and Players Are Fighting Voter Suppression as Election Day Nears." *USA Today*, August 28, 2020. https://www.usatoday.com /story/sports/nba/2020/08/28/nba-fighting-voter-suppression/5598256002.

Mendonca, Rita Duarte, Maria Gouveia-Pereira, and Mariana Miranda. "Belief in a Just World and Secondary Victimization: The Role of Adolescent Deviant Behavior." *Personality and Individual Differences* 97 (2016): 82–87. https://doi .org/10.1016/j.paid.2016.03.021.

Miller, James Andrew, and Tom Shales. *Those Guys Have All the Fun: Inside the World of ESPN.* Boston: Little, Brown, 2021.

Molloy, Parker. "In Defense of Protesters, a Baltimore Orioles Baseball Executive Launched into an Epic Twitter Rant." Upworthy, April 28, 2015. https://www. upworthy.com/in-defense-of-protesters-a-baltimore-orioles-baseball-executive -launched-into-an-epic-twitter-rant.

Montemayor, Constanza. "UCLA's Arthur Ashe Legacy Fund Sponsors Sports Agency Internship for Students." *Daily Bruin*, September 4, 2021. https://dai-lybruin.com/2021/09/04/uclas-arthur-ashe-legacy-fund-sponsors-sports-agency -internship-for-students.

Montgomery, Renee. "An Open Letter to Senator Kelly Loeffler." Medium.com, July 10, 2020. https://medium.com/@itsreneem?p=1af7256698a7.

Morgan, Thad. "Why MLK's Right-Hand Man, Bayard Rustin, Was Nearly Written Out of History." History.com, January 15, 2020. https://www.history.com/news /bayard-rustin-march-on-washington-openly-gay-mlk.

Morrison, Aaron. "Decades Later, A New Look at Black Panthers and Their Legacy." AP News, October 31, 2021. https://apnews.com/article/black-panther-party-huey -newton-race-and-ethnicity-d3cafbc0f7c0f83103f8a5ffaa66faff.

Morse, Ben. "Charlie Sifford: Golf's First Black Professional Who Paved the Way for Tiger Woods." CNN, July 2, 2021. https://www.cnn.com/2021/07/02/golf/charlie -sifford-black-pga-tour-golf-cmd-spc-spt-intl/index.html.

Mossman, John. "Abdul-Rauf Suspended over National Anthem." AP News, March 12, 1996. https://apnews.com/article/0a244b7bf3d7c3882229d7f0e84587d6.

Nadkarni, Rohan, and Alex Nieves. "Why Missouri's Football Team Joined a Protest against School Administration." *Sports Illustrated*, November 9, 2015. https://www.si.com/college/2015/11/09/missouri-football-protest-racism -tim-wolfe.

Nashville SC Communications. "MLS Announces Updates and Enhancements to Diversity Hiring Policy." *Nashville SC*, December 7, 2021. https://www .nashvillesc.com/news/mls-announces-updates-and-enhancements-to-diversity -hiring-policy.

"NBA Board of Governors Launch First-Ever NBA Foundation in Partnership with NBPA to Support Black Communities and Drive Generational Change." NBPA, August 5, 2020. https://nbpa.com/news/nba-board-of-governors-launch-first-ever -nba-foundation-in-partnership-with-nbpa-to-support-black-communities-and -drive-generational-change.

"NBA Legend and Prostate Cancer Survivor Kareem Abdul-Jabbar Featured in New Public Service Announcement by the Prostate Cancer Foundation and NBA Cares Launched on Father's Day." Prostate Cancer Foundation, June 21, 2021. https://www.pcf.org/news/nba-legend-and-prostate-cancer-survivor-kareem -abdul-jabbar-featured-in-new-public-service-announcement-by-the-prostate -cancer-foundation-and-nba-cares.

"NFLPA Files Grievance Challenging NFL's New Anthem Policy; Will Talk to NFL about Situation." NFLPA, July 10, 2018. https://nflpa.com/press/nflpa-files -grievance-challenging-nfl-s-new-anthem-policy-will-talk-to-nfl-about-solution.

"NFLPA Statement on Philadelphia Eagles White House Visit." NFLPA, June 5, 2018. https://nflpa.com/press/nflpa-statement-on-philadelphia-eagles-white-house-visit.

Noriega, Christina. "Black Lives Matter Is Seen as a Trend—It's Time to Wake Up." *Huck*, July 27, 2020. https://www.huckmag.com/perspectives/activism-2 /colombia-black-lives-matter-trend-racism.

North, Anna. "How Racist Policing Took Over American Cities, Explained by a Historian." *Vox*, June, 6, 2020. https://www.vox.com/2020/6/6/21280643/police -brutality-violence-protests-racism-khalil-muhammad.

Northam, Mitchell. "Jackie Robinson: Before the Dodgers, a 4-Sport Start at UCLA." NCAA, April 15, 2020. https://wwwcache.ncaa.com/news/baseball /article/2020-01-31/jackie-robinson-ucla-four-sport-star-notable-moments.

Nwulu, Mac. "Three Journalists Join Jason Whitlock's ESPN Site for African -American Audiences." ESPN, November 18, 2014. https://espnpressroom.com /us/press-releases/2014/11/three-journalists-join-jason-whitlocks-espn-site-for -african-american-audiences.

Owens, Jason. "Roger Goodell: NFL Admits 'We Were Wrong' on Player Protests, Says 'Black Lives Matter.'" Yahoo!, June 5, 2020. https://www.yahoo.com /now/roger-goodell-nfl-admits-we-were-wrong-on-player-protests-black-lives -matter-224540686.html.

Parker, Ryan, and Kimberly Nordyke. "Nike's Polarizing Colin Kaepernick Ad Wins Emmy for Best Commercial." *Hollywood Reporter*, September 15, 2018. https://www.hollywoodreporter.com/news/general-news/nikes-colin-kaepernick -protest-ad-wins-emmy-best-commercial-1239853.

Pawar, Devika. "Nike Air Jordan's Journey from Struggling in the NBA to Making Billions per Year." *Republic World*, updated May 20, 2020. https://www .republicworld.com/sports-news/basketball-news/nike-air-jordans-journey-to -making-billions-per-year-the-last-dance.html.

Pells, Eddie. "Explainer: What's the History of the Olympics Protest Rule?" AP News, July 22, 2021. https://apnews.com/article/2020-tokyo-olympics -explainer-protest-rule-racial-injustice-dcb4de638c59b77d259f713af73f5c5a.

Pells, Eddie, and Pat Graham. "Incredible Raven: Saunders Lends Her Voice to the Olympics." AP News, August 1, 2021. https://apnews.com/article/2020-tokyo -olympics-track-and-field-raven-saunders-769bc8c5816d9a228463c530ff04e1b6.

Peralta, Eyder. "Timeline: What We Know about the Freddie Gray Arrest." NPR, May 1, 2015. https://www.npr.org/sections/thetwo-way/2015/05/01/403629104 /baltimore-protests-what-we-know-about-the-freddie-gray-arrest.

Perez, A. J. "Santa Clara Police Chief Asks Union to Back Off Boycott Threat of 49ers' Home Games." *USA Today*, September 5, 2016. https://www.usatoday.com /story/sports/nfl/49ers/2016/09/03/santa-clara-police-chief-colin-kaepernick-san -francisco-49ers/89835590.

Peter, Josh. "NAACP President: 'Not a Stretch' to Compare Colin Kaepernick to Rosa Parks." *USA Today*, September 8, 2016. https://www.usatoday.com/story /sports/nfl/49ers/2016/09/08/colin-kaepernick-national-anthem-protest-naacp -rosa-parks/90095534.

Pfeiffer, Sacha. "Why the Red Sox Gave Jackie Robinson a 'Tryout' before He Joined the Dodgers." WBUR.org, April 12, 2013. https://www.wbur.org/news/2013/04/12 /jackie-robinson-movie-red-sox.

Picheta, Rob, Nic Robertson, Mick Krever, and Nada Bashir. "Thousands Join Black Lives Matter Protest in London, as Bolted Police Horse Causes Panic." CNN. com, June 8, 2020. https://www.cnn.com/2020/06/06/uk/london-black-lives-matter -protests-saturday-gbr-intl/index.html.

Poon, Kai-Tak, and Zhansheng Chen. "When Justice Surrenders: The Effect of Just-World Beliefs on Aggression Following Ostracism." *Journal of Experimental Social Psychology* 52 (2014): 101–12. https://doi.org/10.1016/j.jesp.2014.01.006.

"QB Colin Kaepernick Files Grievance for Collusion against NFL Owners." ESPN, October 15, 2017. https://www.espn.com/nfl/story/_/id/21035352/colin-kaepernick-files-grievance-nfl-owners-collusion.

Ramos, Miguel R., Isabel Correia, and Helder Alves. "To Believe or Not to Believe in a Just World? The Psychological Costs of Threats to the Belief in a Just World and the Role of Attributions." *Self and Identity* 13, no. 3 (2014): 257–73. https://doi.org/10.1080/15298868.2013.798890.

Reick, Dana. "Gardner Partners with Vera Institute to Reduce Racial Disparities in Legal System." *St. Louis American*, April, 8, 2021. https://www.stlamerican.com/business/business_news/gardner-partners-with-vera-institute-to-reduce-racial-disparities-in-legal-system/article_b9e54fc4-98a8-11eb-b0a5-8bb4ab88394f.html.

Rhodes, Mark Alan, II. "Placing Paul Robeson in History: Understanding His Philosophical Framework." *Journal of Black Studies* 47, no. 3 (2016): 235–57.

Richmond, Todd. "Feds Won't Seek Charges against Cop in Jacob Blake Shooting." AP News, October 10, 2021. https://apnews.com/article/us-news-us-department-of-justice-rusten-sheskey-jacob-blake-kenosha-4f8493dd0776ef6046e052a538cd1460.

Rishe, Patrick. "Oversaturation and Changes in Viewing Habits the Most Likely Explanations for NFL's Ratings Dip." *Forbes*, November 1, 2017. https://www.forbes.com/sites/prishe/2017/11/01/oversaturation-and-changes-in-viewing-habits-the-most-likely-explanations-for-nfls-ratings-dip.

Rogers, Alan. "Passports and Politics: The Courts and the Cold War." *The Historian* 47, no. 4 (1985): 497–511.

Rolley, Bel. "Behind the Jersey: We Must Address the Struggles of Black Women in Soccer." *Daily Trojan*, October 7, 2020. https://dailytrojan.com/2020/10/07/behind-the-jersey-we-must-address-the-struggles-of-black-women-in-soccer.

Rovell, Darren. "NFL Television Ratings Down 9.7 Percent during 2017 Regular Season." ABC News, January 4, 2018. https://abcnews.go.com/Sports/nfl-television-ratings-97-percent-2017-regular-season/story?id=52143709.

Samuels, Allison. "Rodney King's Legacy." *Daily Beast*, updated July 13, 2017. https://www.thedailybeast.com/rodney-kings-legacy.

Sarat, Austin. "Review: Authority, Anxiety, and Procedural Justice: Moving from Scientific Detachment to Critical Engagement." *Law & Society Review* 27, no. 3 (1993): 647–71. https://doi.org/10.2307/3054110.

Schad, Tom. "Donald Trump: No White House Invitation for Cavs' LeBron James, Warriors' Steph Curry or Teams." *USA Today*, June 8, 2018. https://www.usatoday.com/story/sports/nba/2018/06/08/donald-trump-lebron-james-steph-curry-not-invited-white-house/684154002.

Schaefer, Rob. "What December Start, Shortened Schedule in '21 Means for NBA." NBC Sports, October 23, 2020. https://www.nbcsports.com/chicago/bulls/reports-nba-targeting-december-start-date-shortened-regular-season.

Schmittel, Annelie, and Jimmy Sanderson. "Talking about Trayvon in 140 Characters: Exploring NFL Player's Tweets about the George Zimmerman Verdict." *Journal of Sport & Social Issues* 39, no. 4 (2015): 332–45. https://doi:10.1177/0193723514557821.

Schouten, Fredreka. "Here's Why Voting Rights Activists Say Georgia's New Election Law Targets Black Voters." CNN, updated March 26, 2021. https://www.cnn .com/2021/03/26/politics/georgia-voting-law-black-voters/index.html.

Schroth, Raymond A. "Journey into the Mysteries of Paul Robeson." *National Catholic Reporter*, September 12, 2018. https://www.ncronline.org/news/people /journey-mysteries-paul-robeson.

Sherman, Rodger. "Everything about That Missouri Bill to Ban College Athletes from Protesting Was Stupid." *SB Nation*, December 16, 2015. https://www.sbnation .com/2015/12/16/10214874/missouri-bill-athletes-protest-rick-brattin.

Silva, Cynthia. "Costa Rican Gymnast, an Olympic First, Lauded for Black Lives Matter Tribute." NBC News, updated July 26, 2021. https://www.nbcnews.com /news/latino/costa-rican-gymnast-olympic-first-lauded-black-lives-matter-tribute -rcna1515.

Silver, Johnathan. "Texas Gov. Abbott Signs 'Sandra Bland Act' into Law." *Texas Tribune*, June 15, 2017. https://www.texastribune.org/2017/06/15/texas-gov-greg -abbott-signs-sandra-bland-act-law.

Simon, Scott. "'Ol' Man River': An American Masterpiece." NPR, May 31, 2003. https://www.npr.org/2003/05/31/1279965/ol-man-river-an-american-masterpiece.

Sims, Alexandra. "Muhammad Ali: Why Did the Boxing Legend Change His Name from Cassius Clay?" *Independent*, June 4, 2016. https://www.independent.co.uk /news/people/muhammad-ali-death-cassius-clay-why-did-he-change-his-name -nation-islam-a7065256.html.

Smith, Johnny. "Jackie Robinson Was Asked to Denounce Paul Robeson. Instead, He Went after Jim Crow." *Andscape*, April 15, 2019. https://andscape.com /features/jackie-robinson-was-asked-to-denounce-paul-robeson-before-huac -instead-he-went-after-jim-crow.

Smith, Rodney K. "A Brief History of the National Collegiate Athletic Association's Role in Regulating Intercollegiate Athletics." *Marquette Sports Law Review* 11, no. 1 (2000): 5.

"Social Welfare Organizations." IRS.gov, accessed November 26, 2021. https://www .irs.gov/charities-non-profits/other-non-profits/social-welfare-organizations.

Sokolowski, Alexandra. "May 26, 1956: The Day Althea Gibson Became the First Black Player to Win a Grand Slam." Tennis Majors, May 26, 2021. https://www .tennismajors.com/our-features/may-26th-1956-the-day-althea-gibson-became -the-first-black-player-to-win-a-grand-slam-260009.html.

Sprigle, Ray. *In the Land of Jim Crow*. New York: Simon and Schuster, 1949.

Stevens, Matthew. "NFL Inks a 10-Year Stadium Partnership with Tottenham Hotspurs." *Baltimore Beatdown*, July 8, 2015. https://www.baltimorebeatdown .com/2015/7/8/8913305/nfl-inks-a-10-year-stadium-partnership-with-tottenham -hotspurs.

Streeter, Kurt. "In Inglewood, Optimism and Anxiety Neighbor Super Bowl Stadium." *New York Times*, updated February 13, 2022. https://www.nytimes .com/2022/02/10/sports/football/where-is-the-super-bowl-2022.html.

Suddler, Carl. "George Floyd Changed the World of Athlete Activism." *Washington Post*, May 25, 2021. https://www.washingtonpost.com/outlook/2021/05/25/george -floyd-changed-world-athlete-activism.

Sullivan, Emily. "Laura Ingraham Told LeBron James to Shut Up and Dribble; He Went to the Hoop." NPR, February 19, 2018. https://www.npr.org/sections /thetwo-way/2018/02/19/587097707/laura-ingraham-told-lebron-james-to-shutup -and-dribble-he-went-to-the-hoop.

Tennery, Amy. "Most Americans Disagree with Kaepernick, But Respect His Right to Protest." Reuters, September 14, 2016. https://www.reuters.com/article/us-nfl -anthem-poll-idUSKCN11K2ID.

Thompson, Debra, and Chloe Thurston. "American Development of the Black Lives Matter." In *The Politics of Protest: Readings on the Black Lives Matter Movement*, edited by Nadia E. Brown, Ray Block Jr., and Christopher Stout, 1–4. Abington: Routledge, 2021.

Toosi, Nahal. "Obama Asks Kaepernick to Think about Pain He's Causing Military Families." *Politico*, September 28, 2016. https://www.politico.com/story/2016/09 /obama-colin-kaepernick-anthem-228880.

Treisman, Rachel. "The U.S. National Women's Soccer Team Wins $24 Million in Equal Pay Settlement." NPR, February 22, 2022. https://www.npr .org/2022/02/22/1082272202/women-soccer-contracts-equal-pay-settlement -uswnt.

Trendafiova, Sylvia, Vassilios Ziakas, and Emily Sparvero. "Linking Corporate Social Responsibility in Sport with Community Development: An Added Source of Community Value." *Sport in Society* 20, no. 7 (2017): 938—956. https://doi.org /10.1080/17430437.2016.1221935.

Truong, Debbie. "D.C. Finishes Construction on Black Lives Matter Plaza." *DCist*, October 28, 2021. https://dcist.com/story/21/10/28/dc-finishes-construction-on -black-lives-matter-plaza.

Under Armour. "Black Lives Matter." Twitter, June 2, 2020. https://twitter.com /underarmour/status/1267860290642808832.

"Universal Negro Improvement Association." PBS, accessed November 13, 2021. https://www.chicagomanualofstyle.org/tools_citationguide/citation-guide-1.html.

Vredenburg, Jessica, Amanda Spry, Joya Kemper, and Sommer Kapitan. "Athlete Activism or Corporate Woke Washing? Getting It Right in the Age of Black Lives Matter Is a Tough Game." *The Conversation*, September 20, 2020. https://theconversation.com/athlete-activism-or-corporate-woke-washing-getting -it-right-in-the-age-of-black-lives-matter-is-a-tough-game-146301.

Wade, Reggie. "Nike, Michael Jordan Commit $140 million to Support the Black Community." *Yahoo!*, June 5, 2020. https://www.yahoo.com/now/nike-commits -40-million-to-support-the-black-community-135747947.html.

Walker, Rhiannon. "Althea Gibson, Arthur Ashe Highlight a Century of ATA Champions." *The Undefeated*, August 4, 2017. https://theundefeated.com/features/althea -gibson-arthur-ashe-highlight-a-century-of-ata-champions.

Wartenberg, Steve. "In the News World of NIL, Luke Fedlam Guides Athletes on Money, Deals, and the Future." Columbus CEO, updated July 3, 2021.

https://www.columbusceo.com/story/business/briefs/2021/07/01/college-athletes
-and-nil-luke-fedlam-trusted-adviser/7577807002.

"Washington Mystics Organize WNBA Teams to 'Unite the Vote' in a Voter Registration Challenge." Mystics.WNBA.com, August 18, 2020. https://mystics.wnba.com/news /washington-mystics-organize-wnba-teams-to-unite-the-vote-in-a-voter-registration -challenge.

Watkins, Eli. "Pence Leaves Colts Game after Protest during Anthem." CNN, October 9, 2017. https://www.cnn.com/2017/10/08/politics/vice-president-mike-pence-nfl -protest/index.html.

Wilf, Steve. "Athletes and Activism: The Long, Defiant History of Sports Protests." *The Undefeated*, January 30, 2019. https://theundefeated.com/features/athletes -and-activism-the-long-defiant-history-of-sports-protests.

Winfield, Kristian. "Stephen Curry Supports Skipping White House Visit, Hopes It Will 'Inspire Some Change.'" *SBNation*, September 22, 2017. https://www .sbnation.com/2017/9/22/16352408/stephen-curry-white-house-visit-warriors -donald-trump-kevin-durant.

Wise, Mike. "Clenched Fists, Helping Hand." *Washington Post*, October 5, 2006. https://www.washingtonpost.com/wp-dyn/content/article/2006/10/04/ AR2006100401753.html.

"WNBA Announces a 2020 Season Dedicated to Social Justice." WNBA.com, July 6, 2020. https://www.wnba.com/news/wnba-announces-a-2020-season-dedicated -to-social-justice.

Wolf, Karen. "From *Plessy v. Ferguson* to *Brown v. Board of Education*: The Supreme Court Rules on School Desegregation." Yale-New Haven Teachers Institute, accessed November 13, 2021. https://teachersinstitute.yale.edu/pubs/A5/wolff.html.

Wyche, Steve. "Colin Kaepernick Explains Why He Sat during National Anthem." NFL.com, August 27, 2016. https://www.nfl.com/news/colin-kaepernick-explains -why-he-sat-during-national-anthem-0ap3000000691077.

Yaffa, Joshua. "A Black Communist's Disappearance in Stalin's Russia." *New Yorker*, October 18, 2021. https://www.newyorker.com/magazine/2021/10/25/a-black -communists-disappearance-in-stalins-russia-lovett-fort-whiteman-gulag.

Yates, Clinton. "Colin Kaepernick Covers 'TIME' Magazine." *The Undefeated*, September 22, 2016. https://theundefeated.com/whhw/colin-kaepernick-covers -time-magazine.

Yglesias, Matthew. "Donald Sterling's Racist Outbursts." *Vox*, updated May 13, 2015. https://www.vox.com/2014/4/29/18077046/donald-sterling.

Yokley, Eli. "29% GOP Voters Say It's Likely Trump Will Be Reinstated as President This Year." Morning Consult, June 9, 2021. https://morningconsult .com/2021/06/09/trump-reinstated-democracy-polling.

Young, Jabari. "LA Clippers Sign $300-Million-Plus Arena Sponsorship Deal with Green Bank Aspiration." CNBC, September 27, 2021. https://www.cnbc .com/2021/09/27/la-clippers-aspiration-sign-300-million-plus-arena-sponsor-deal. html.

Yuen, Nancy Wang. "How Racial Stereotypes in Popular Media Affect People— and What Hollywood Can Do to Become More Inclusive." *Scholars*, June 4,

2019. https://scholars.org/contribution/how-racial-stereotypes-popular-media-affect -people-and-what-hollywood-can-do-become.

Zirin, David. "Fists of Freedom: An Olympic Story Not Taught in School." PBS, accessed November 13, 2021. https://www.pbs.org/newshour/extra/app /uploads/2014/02/All-docs-for-Human-Rights-lesson-2.pdf.

Notes

INTRODUCTION

1. John Mossman, "Abdul-Rauf Suspended over National Anthem," AP News, March 12, 1996, https://apnews.com/article/0a244b7bf3d7c3882229d7f0e84587d6.

CHAPTER ONE

1. "Universal Negro Improvement Association," PBS, accessed November 13, 2021, https://www.chicagomanualofstyle.org/tools_citationguide/citation-guide-1.html.

2. Mark Christian, "Marcus Garvey and African Unity: Lessons for the Future from the Past," *Journal of Black Studies* 39, no. 2 (2008): 316–31.

3. Jabez Ayodele Langley, "Garveyism and African Nationalism," *Race & Class* 11, no. 2 (1969): 157–72.

4. Chris Lamb, "When a Black Boxing Champion Beat the 'Great White Hope,' All Hell Broke Loose," *The Conversation*, June 30, 2021, https://theconversation.com/when-a-Black-boxing-champion-beat-the-great-white-hope-all-hell-broke-loose-163413.

5. Gilbert King, "What Paul Robeson Said," *Smithsonian*, September 13, 2011, https://www.smithsonianmag.com/history/what-paul-robeson-said-77742433.

6. Scott Simon, "'Ol' Man River': An American Masterpiece," NPR, May 31, 2003, https://www.npr.org/2003/05/31/1279965/ol-man-river-an-american-masterpiece.

7. Joshua Yaffa, "A Black Communist's Disappearance in Stalin's Russia," *New Yorker*, October 18, 2021, https://www.newyorker.com/magazine/2021/10/25/a-Black-communists-disappearance-in-stalins-russia-lovett-fort-whiteman-gulag.

8. Jenny Farrell, "Paul Robeson: Activist, Communist, and Spokesperson for the Oppressed of the Earth," *Culture Matters*, March 31, 2018, https://www.culturematters.org.uk/index.php/arts/music/item/2772-paul-robeson-activist-and-spokesperson-for-the-oppressed.

9. Raymond A. Schroth, "Journey into the Mysteries of Paul Robeson," *National Catholic Reporter*, September 12, 2018, https://www.ncronline.org/news/people/journey-mysteries-paul-robeson.

10. Alan Rogers, "Passports and Politics: The Courts and the Cold War," *The Historian* 47, no. 4 (1985): 497–511.

11. Mark Alan Rhodes II, "Placing Paul Robeson in History: Understanding His Philosophical Framework," *Journal of Black Studies* 47, no. 3 (2016): 235–57.

12. Sacha Pfeiffer, "Why the Red Sox Gave Jackie Robinson a 'Tryout' before He Joined the Dodgers," WBUR.org, April 12, 2013, https://www.wbur.org/news/2013/04/12/jackie-robinson-movie-red-sox.

13. Johnny Smith, "Jackie Robinson Was Asked to Denounce Paul Robeson. Instead, He Went after Jim Crow," *Andscape*, April 15, 2019, https://andscape.com/features/jackie-robinson-was-asked-to-denounce-paul-robeson-before-huac-instead-he-went-after-jim-crow.

14. Brigit Katz, "Althea Gibson, Who Smashed through Racial Barriers in Tennis, Honored with Statue at U.S. Open," *Smithsonian*, August 28, 2019, https://www.smithsonianmag.com/smart-news/althea-gibson-who-smashed-through-racial-barriers-tennis-honored-statue-us-open-180973001.

15. Rhiannon Walker, "Althea Gibson, Arthur Ashe Highlight a Century of ATA Champions," *The Undefeated*, August 4, 2017, https://theundefeated.com/features/althea-gibson-arthur-ashe-highlight-a-century-of-ata-champions.

16. Alicia Ault, "Althea Gibson's Momentous Achievement," *Smithsonian*, June 1, 2021, https://www.smithsonianmag.com/smithsonian-institution/sixty-five-years-ago-althea-gibson-broke-color-line-french-open-180977859.

17. Frances Clayton Gray and Yanick Lamb, *Born to Win: The Authorized Biography of Althea Gibson* (Hoboken, NJ: Wiley, 2004).

18. Ben Morse, "Charlie Sifford: Golf's First Black Professional Who Paved the Way for Tiger Woods," CNN, July 2, 2021, https://www.cnn.com/2021/07/02/golf/charlie-sifford-Black-pga-tour-golf-cmd-spc-spt-intl/index.html.

19. Mark Cannizzaro, "Charlie Sifford, the Jackie Robinson of Golf, Dead at 92," *New York Post*, February 4, 2015, https://nypost.com/2015/02/04/charlie-sifford-the-jackie-robinson-of-golf-dead-at-92.

20. Jason Gay, "Muhammad Ali Shook Up the World," *Wall Street Journal*, updated June 4, 2016, https://www.wsj.com/articles/muhammad-ali-shook-up-the-world-1465022480.

21. Shaddi Abusaid, "Muhammad Ali's Return to the Ring Electrified Atlanta, Black Community," *Atlanta Journal-Constitution*, February 24, 2020, https://www.ajc.com/lifestyles/muhammad-ali-return-the-ring-electrified-atlanta-black-community/S22y8j0zLW7K4iGSPuOD8H.

22. David Zirin, "Fists of Freedom: An Olympic Story Not Taught in School," PBS, accessed November 13, 2021, https://www.pbs.org/newshour/extra/app /uploads/2014/02/All-docs-for-Human-Rights-lesson-2.pdf.

23. "Arthur Ashe," *Biography*, accessed November 13, 2021, https://www .biography.com/athlete/arthur-ashe.

24. Devika Pawar, "Nike Air Jordan's Journey from Struggling in the NBA to Making Billions per Year," *Republic World*, updated May 20, 2020, https://www .republicworld.com/sports-news/basketball-news/nike-air-jordans-journey-to -making-billions-per-year-the-last-dance.html.

CHAPTER TWO

1. Lois Elfman, "Black Male Student-Athletes Still Face Harsh Inequities," Diverse Education, March 11, 2018, https://www.diverseeducation.com/home /article/15102161/black-male-student-athletes-still-face-harsh-inequities.

2. Zach Dirlam, "There's No Crying in College: The Case against Paying College Athletes," *Bleacher Report*, April, 2, 2013, https://bleacherreport.com /articles/1588301-theres-no-crying-in-college-the-case-against-paying-college -athletes.

3. George B. Cunningham and Michael R. Regan Jr., "Political Activism, racial Identity and the Commercial Endorsement of Athletes," *International Review for the Sociology of Sport* 47, no. 6 (2012): 657–69, https://doi.org/10.1177/1012690211416358.

4. Jim Euchner, "The Medium Is the Message," *Research-Technology Management* 59, no. 5 (2016): 9–11, https://doi.org/10.1080/08956308.2016.1209068.

5. Paul Bond, "Study: TV Violence Linked to 'Mean World Syndrome,'" *Hollywood Reporter*, June 18, 2014, https://www.hollywoodreporter.com/news/general -news/study-tv-violence-linked-mean-712890.

6. Rayeheh Alitvavoli and Ehsan Kaveh, "The U.S. Media's Effect on Public's Crime Expectations: A Cycle of Cultivation and Agenda-Setting Theory," *Societies* 8, no. 58 (Summer 2018): 2–9, https://doi:10.3390/soc8030058.

7. Annelie Schmittel and Jimmy Sanderson, "Talking about Trayvon in 140 Characters: Exploring NFL Players' Tweets about the George Zimmerman Verdict," *Journal of Sport and Social Issues* 39, no. 4 (2014): 1–14, https://doi.org/10.1177/0193723514557821.

8. Matthew Yglesias, "Donald Sterling's Racist Outbursts," *Vox*, updated May 13, 2015, https://www.vox.com/2014/4/29/18077046/donald-sterling.

9. Steve Wilf, "Athletes and Activism: The Long, Defiant History of Sports Protests," *The Undefeated*, January 30, 2019, https://theundefeated.com/features /athletes-and-activism-the-long-defiant-history-of-sports-protests.

10. Emmitt L. Gill Jr., "Hands Up, Don't Shoot or Shut Up and Play Ball? Fan -Generated Media Views of the Ferguson Five," *Journal of Human Behavior in the Social Environment* 26, nos. 3–4 (2016): 400–412, https://doi.org/10.1080/10911359 .2016.1139990.

11. Mike Florio, "St. Louis Police Officers Association Condemns Rams' Ferguson Gesture," *Pro Football Talk*, November 30, 2014, https://profootballtalk.nbcsports.com/2014/11/30/st-louis-police-officers-association-condemns-rams-ferguson-gesture.

12. Tom Gatto, "Police, Rams Can't Agree on Definition of 'Apology,'" *Sporting News*, January 12, 2014, https://www.sportingnews.com/au/nfl/news/hands-up-don-t-shoot-st-louis-rams-ferguson-protests-kevin-demoff-apology-st-louis-police-slpoa/kgjkcjkh0sfz16mvtqiqz4qrv.

13. J. A. Adande, "Purpose of I Can't Breathe T-Shirts," ESPN, December 10, 2014, https://www.espn.com/nba/story/_/id/12010612/nba-stars-making-statement-wearing-breathe-shirts.

14. John Breech, "Browns Refuse Apology to Cleveland Cops over Andrew Hawkins' Actions," CBS Sports, December 15, 2014, https://www.cbssports.com/nfl/news/browns-refuse-apology-to-cleveland-cops-over-andrew-hawkins-actions.

15. Pat McManamon, "Police Decry Andrew Hawkins Protest," ESPN, December 14, 2014, https://www.espn.com/nfl/story/_/id/12030748/andrew-hawkins-cleveland-browns-wears-protest-shirt-police-seek-apology.

16. Elizabeth Day, "#BlackLivesMatter: The Birth of a New Civil Rights Movement," *Guardian*, July 19, 2015, https://www.theguardian.com/world/2015/jul/19/Blacklivesmatter-birth-civil-rights-movement.

17. Kristine Nicole Dukes and Sarah E. Gaither, "Black Racial Stereotypes and Victim Blaming: Implications for Media Coverage and Criminal Proceedings in Cases of Police Violence against Racial and Ethnic Minorities," *Journal of Social Issues* 73, no. 4 (2017): 789–807, https://doi.org/10.1111.josi.12248.

18. Danielle Kilgo and Rache R. Mourao, "Media Effects and Marginalized Ideas: Relationships among Media Consumption and Support for Black Lives Matter," *International Journal of Communication* 13 (2019): 4287–305.

19. Debra Thompson and Chloe Thurston, "American Development of the Black Lives Matter," in *The Politics of Protest: Readings on the Black Lives Matter Movement*, ed. Nadia E. Brown, Ray Block Jr., and Christopher Stout, 1–4 (Abington: Routledge, 2021).

20. Melvin J. Lerner, *The Belief in a Just World: A Fundamental Delusion* (Boston: Springer, 1980).

21. Miguel R. Ramos, Isabel Correia, and Helder Alves, "To Believe or Not to Believe in a Just World? The Psychological Costs of Threats to the Belief in a Just World and the Role of Attributions," *Self and Identity* 13, no. 3 (2014): 257–73, https://doi.org/10.1080/15298868.2013.798890.

22. Claire Andre and Manuel Velasquez, "The Just World Theory," *Issues in Ethics* (Markkula Center for Applied Ethics) 3, no. 2 (Spring 1990).

23. Ray Sprigle, *In the Land of Jim Crow* (New York: Simon and Schuster, 1949).

24. Steve Knopper, "The True Story of N.W.A. Playing 'Fuck the Police' Live in Detroit," *GQ*, July 21, 2020, https://www.gq.com/story/nwa-fuck-the-police-live-detroit.

25. Mac Nwulu, "Three Journalists Join Jason Whitlock's ESPN Site for African-American Audiences," ESPN, November 18, 2014, https://espnpressroom

.com/us/press-releases/2014/11/three-journalists-join-jason-whitlocks-espn-site-for-african-american-audiences.

26. Jonah Engel Bromwich, "Michael Jordan Says He Is 'Deeply Troubled' by Recent Police-Related Violence," *New York Times*, July 25, 2016, https://www.nytimes.com/2016/07/26/sports/basketball/michael-jordan-statement-on-police-related-violence.html.

27. Rohan Nadkarni and Alex Nieves, "Why Missouri's Football Team Joined a Protest against School Administration," *Sports Illustrated*, November 9, 2015, https://www.si.com/college/2015/11/09/missouri-football-protest-racism-tim-wolfe.

28. Zellie Imani, "Everything You Need to Know about the Students' Demands ahead of #StudentBlackOut National Day of Action," *Atlanta Black Star*, November 18, 2015, https://atlantaBlackstar.com/2015/11/18/everything-you-need-to-know-about-the-students-demands-ahead-of-studentBlackout-national-day-of-action.

29. Rodger Sherman, "Everything about That Missouri Bill to Ban College Athletes from Protesting Was Stupid," *SB Nation*, December 16, 2015, https://www.sbnation.com/2015/12/16/10214874/missouri-bill-athletes-protest-rick-brattin.

CHAPTER THREE

1. Steve Wyche, "Colin Kaepernick Explains Why He Sat during National Anthem," NFL.com, August 27, 2016, https://www.nfl.com/news/colin-kaepernick-explains-why-he-sat-during-national-anthem-0ap3000000691077.

2. Wyche, "Colin Kaepernick Explains."

3. Cindy Boren, "Arian Foster and Three Dolphins Teammates Protest during National Anthem Protest," *Washington Post*, September 11, 2016, https://www.washingtonpost.com/news/early-lead/wp/2016/09/11/arian-foster-and-three-dolphins-teammates-protest-during-national-anthem.

4. Amy Tennery, "Most Americans Disagree with Kaepernick but Respect His Right to Protest," Reuters, September 14, 2016, https://www.reuters.com/article/us-nfl-anthem-poll-idUSKCN11K2ID.

5. Nahal Toosi, "Obama Asks Kaepernick to Think about the Pain He's Causing Military Families," *Politico*, September 28, 2016, https://www.politico.com/story/2016/09/obama-colin-kaepernick-anthem-228880.

6. Andrew Blankstein and Danielle Silva, "LeBron James' Los Angeles Home Vandalized with 'N-Word' Graffiti," NBC News, updated June 1, 2017, https://www.nbcnews.com/news/us-news/lebron-james-los-angeles-home-vandalized-n-word-graffiti-n766651.

7. Will Brinson, "The 49ers Would've Cut Colin Kaepernick If He Hadn't Opted Out of His Contract," CBS Sports, May 31, 2017, https://www.cbssports.com/nfl/news/the-49ers-wouldve-cut-colin-kaepernick-if-he-hadnt-opted-out-of-his-contract.

8. Alexa Lardieri, "Trump to Hannity: You Can't Disrespect Our Flag," *U.S. News*, October 12, 2017, https://www.usnews.com/news/politics/articles/2017-10-12/trump-to-hannity-you-cant-disrespect-our-flag.

9. John Breech, "Roger Goodell Calls Out Donald Trump for Making 'Divisive Comments' about the NFL," CBS Sports, September 23, 2017, https://www.cbssports.com/nfl/news/roger-goodell-calls-out-donald-trump-for-making-divisive-comments-about-the-nfl.

10. Darren Rovell, "NFL Television Ratings Down 9.7 Percent during 2017 Regular Season," ABC News, January 4, 2018, https://abcnews.go.com/Sports/nfl-television-ratings-97-percent-2017-regular-season/story?id=52143709.

11. Richard Deitsch, "Why the NFL's Ratings Saw a Steep Decline in 2017," *Sports Illustrated*, January 3, 2018, https://www.si.com/media/2018/01/03/nfl-ratings-decline-espn-fox-nbc-network-tv.

12. Eli Watkins, "Pence Leaves Colts Game after Protest during Anthem," CNN, October 9, 2017, https://www.cnn.com/2017/10/08/politics/vice-president-mike-pence-nfl-protest/index.html.

13. "QB Colin Kaepernick Files Grievance for Collusion against NFL Owners," ESPN, October 15, 2017, https://www.espn.com/nfl/story/_/id/21035352/colin-kaepernick-files-grievance-nfl-owners-collusion.

14. "Houston Texans Owner Bob McNair Apologizes for Remark," NFL.com, October 27, 2017, https://www.nfl.com/news/houston-texans-owner-bob-mcnair-apologizes-for-remark-0ap3000000868160.

15. Austin Knoblauch, "NFL Owners Approve National Anthem Policy for 2018," NFL.com, May 23, 2018, https://www.nfl.com/news/nfl-owners-approve-national-anthem-policy-for-2018-0ap3000000933971.

16. Tadd Haislop, "What Is the NFL's National Anthem Protest Policy? Here Are the Rules for Kneeling in 2020," *Sporting News*, September 20, 2020, https://www.sportingnews.com/us/nfl/news/nfl-national-anthem-policy-2020-kneeling-protests/1o88fwivdxvqu1d8nnbiw5dw3z.

17. "NFLPA Files Grievance Challenging NFL's New Anthem Policy; Will Talk to NFL about Situation," NFLPA, July 10, 2018, https://nflpa.com/press/nflpa-files-grievance-challenging-nfl-s-new-anthem-policy-will-talk-to-nfl-about-solution.

18. Kristian Winfield, "Stephen Curry Supports Skipping White House Visit, Hopes It Will 'Inspire Some Change,'" *SBNation*, September 22, 2017, https://www.sbnation.com/2017/9/22/16352408/stephen-curry-white-house-visit-warriors-donald-trump-kevin-durant.

19. "NFLPA Statement on Philadelphia Eagles White House Visit," NFLPA, June 5, 2018, https://nflpa.com/press/nflpa-statement-on-philadelphia-eagles-white-house-visit.

20. Emily Sullivan, "Laura Ingraham Told LeBron James to Shut Up and Dribble; He Went to the Hoop," NPR, February 19, 2018, https://www.npr.org/sections/thetwo-way/2018/02/19/587097707/laura-ingraham-told-lebron-james-to-shutup-and-dribble-he-went-to-the-hoop.

21. Marc Edelman, "Explaining Eric Reid's Collusion Grievance against the NFL," *Forbes*, May 3, 2018, https://www.forbes.com/sites/marcedelman/2018/05/03/explaining-eric-reids-collusion-grievance-against-the-nfl.

22. Eli Yokley, "29% GOP Voters Say It's Likely Trump Will Be Reinstated as President This Year," Morning Consult, June 9, 2021, https://morningconsult .com/2021/06/09/trump-reinstated-democracy-polling.

CHAPTER FOUR

1. "Know Your Rights Camp 10 Points," Know Your Rights Camp, accessed November 30, 2021, https://www.knowyourrightscamp.com/who-we-are.

2. "Social Welfare Organizations," IRS.gov, accessed November 26, 2021, https://www.irs.gov/charities-non-profits/other-non-profits/social-welfare-organizations.

3. Tim Daniels, "Report: NFL, Players Coalition Finalize $90M Social Justice Partnership," *Bleacher Report*, May 22, 2018, https://bleacherreport.com /articles/2777275-report-nfl-players-coalition-finalize-90m-social-justice-partnership.

4. Ryan Parker and Kimberly Nordyke, "Nike's Polarizing Colin Kaepernick Ad Wins Emmy for Best Commercial," *Hollywood Reporter*, September 15, 2018, https://www.hollywoodreporter.com/news/general-news/nikes-colin-kaepernick-pro-test-ad-wins-emmy-best-commercial-1239853.

5. Christina Noriega, "Black Lives Matter Is Seen as a Trend—It's Time to Wake Up," *Huck*, July 27, 2020, https://www.huckmag.com/perspectives/activism-2/colombia -Black-lives-matter-trend-racism.

6. Carl Suddler, "George Floyd Changed the World of Athlete Activism," *Washington Post*, May 25, 2021, https://www.washingtonpost.com/outlook/2021/05/25 /george-floyd-changed-world-athlete-activism.

7. "WNBA Announces a 2020 Season Dedicated to Social Justice," WNBA. com, July 6, 2020, https://www.wnba.com/news/wnba-announces-a-2020-season -dedicated-to-social-justice.

8. Jason Owens, "Roger Goodell: NFL Admits 'We Were Wrong' on Player Protests, Says 'Black Lives Matter,'" Yahoo!, June 5, 2020, https://www.yahoo. com/now/roger-goodell-nfl-admits-we-were-wrong-on-player-protests-Black-lives -matter-224540686.html.

9. "NBA Board of Governors Launch First-Ever NBA Foundation in Partnership with NBPA to Support Black Communities and Drive Generational Change," NBPA, August 5, 2020, https://nbpa.com/news/nba-board-of-governors-launch-first-ever- nba-foundation-in-partnership-with-nbpa-to-support-Black-communities-and-drive -generational-change.

10. Tyler Conway, "NBA Foundation Announce $3M+ in Grants to Support Black Economic Empowerment," *Bleacher Report*, April 5, 2021, https://bleacherre-port.com/articles/2939352-nba-foundation-announce-3m-in-grants-to-support-Black -economic-empowerment.

11. Mark Medina, "How NBA Teams and Players Are Fighting Voter Suppression as Election Day Nears," *USA Today*, August 28, 2020, https://www.usatoday.com /story/sports/nba/2020/08/28/nba-fighting-voter-suppression/5598256002.

12. "Washington Mystics Organize WNBA Teams to 'Unite the Vote' in a Voter Registration Challenge," Mystics.WNBA.com, August 18, 2020, https://mystics

.wnba.com/news/washington-mystics-organize-wnba-teams-to-unite-the-vote-in-a
-voter-registration-challenge.

13. Guardian Sport, "Senator Loeffler Objects to WNBA's Black Lives Matter
Tie-in 'Removal of Jesus,'" The Guardian, July 7, 2020, https://www.theguardian.com
/sport/2020/jul/07/kelly-loeffler-Black-lives-matter-wnba-atlanta-dream.

14. Renee Montgomery, "An Open Letter to Senator Kelly Loeffler," Medium.
com, July 10, 2020, https://medium.com/@itsreneem?p=1af7256698a7.

15. Wilton Jackson, "Zlatan Ibrahimovic: LeBron James, Other Athletes Should
'Do What You're Good At,' Stay Out of Politics," *Sports Illustrated*, February
26, 2021, https://www.si.com/soccer/2021/02/26/zlatan-ibrahimovic-lebron-james
-lakers-athlete-activism-politics.

16. Aris Folley, "LeBron James Responds to Criticism: 'I Would Never Shut
Up about Things That Are Wrong,'" *The Hill*, February 28, 2021, https://thehill.
com/blogs/in-the-know/in-the-know/540872-lebron-james-responds-to-criticism-i
-would-never-shut-up-about.

17. Sean Gentile, "The Steelers' Political Machine and the PAC
Supporting Pittsburgh Candidates," The Athletic, October 29, 2020, https://theathletic
.com/2167116/2020/10/29/pittsburgh-steelers-pac-nfl-political-donations.

18. Fredreka Schouten, "Here's Why Voting Rights Activists Say Georgia's New
Election Law Targets Black Voters," CNN, updated March 26, 2021, https://www
.cnn.com/2021/03/26/politics/georgia-voting-law-black-voters/index.html.

19. Bob Harig, "Masters Chairman Fred Ridley against Boycott over Georgia
Voting Law," ESPN, April 7, 2021, https://www.espn.com/golf/story/_/id/31210086
/masters-chairman-fred-ridley-burdening-augusta-boycott-georgia-voting-law.

20. Dave Fredrickson, "The NFL's Reversal on 'Race Norming' Reveals How Pervasive Medical Racism Remains," NBC News, June 8, 2021, https://www.nbcnews
.com/think/opinion/nfl-s-reversal-race-norming-reveals-how-pervasive-medical
-racism-ncna1269992.

21. Jessica Vredenburg, Amanda Spry, Joya Kemper, and Sommer Kapitan, "Athlete Activism or Corporate Woke Washing? Getting It Right in the Age of Black Lives
Matter Is a Tough Game," *The Conversation*, September 20, 2020, https://theconver-
sation.com/athlete-activism-or-corporate-woke-washing-getting-it-right-in-the-age
-of-Black-lives-matter-is-a-tough-game-146301.

22. Under Armour, "Black Lives Matter," Twitter, June 2, 2020, https://twitter
.com/underarmour/status/1267860290642808832.

23. Reggie Wade, "Nike, Michael Jordan Commit $140 Million to Support
the Black Community," Yahoo!, June 5, 2020, https://www.yahoo.com/now/nike
-commits-40-million-to-support-the-Black-community-135747947.html.

24. Karen Given, "Walter Byers: The Man Who Built the NCAA, then Tried to Tear
It Down," WBUR, October 13, 2017, https://www.wbur.org/onlyagame/2017/10/13
/walter-byers-ncaa.

25. Steve Berkowitz, "Proposed California Bill Could Create New Pressure
in NCAA Name, Image, and Likeness Debate," *USA Today*, updated December
8, 2020, https://www.usatoday.com/story/sports/college/2020/12/07/ncaa-could-face
-pressure-new-california-name-image-likeness-bill/3856850001.

26. "It's Time for a Racial Reckoning in College Sports: Knight Commission Releases Plan to Create Racial Equity for Black College Athletes," Knight Commission, May 12, 2021, https://www.knightcommission.org/2021/05/racial-equity.

27. Eddie Pells, "Explainer: What's the History of the Olympics Protest Rule?," AP News, July 22, 2021, https://apnews.com/article/2020-tokyo-olympics-explainer -protest-rule-racial-injustice-dcb4de638c59b77d259f713af73f5c5a.

28. Pells, "Explainer."

29. Gawon Bae and Jill Martin, "International Olympic Committee Suspends Its Action on Raven Saunders' Podium Protest after Her Mother's Death," CNN, updated August 4, 2021, https://www.cnn.com/2021/08/04/sport/olympian-raven-saunders -protest-action-suspended/index.html.

30. Eddie Pells and Pat Graham, "Incredible Raven: Saunders Lends Her Voice to the Olympics," AP News, August 1, 2021, https://apnews.com/article/2020-tokyo -olympics-track-and-field-raven-saunders-769bc8c5816d9a228463c530ff04e1b6.

CHAPTER FIVE

1. John S. Adams, "Toward an Understanding of Inequity," *Journal of Abnormal and Social Psychology* 67, no. 5 (1963): 422–36, https://doi.org/10.1037/h0040968.

2. Austin Sarat, "Review: Authority, Anxiety, and Procedural Justice: Moving from Scientific Detachment to Critical Engagement," *Law & Society Review* 27, no. 3 (1993): 647–71, https://doi.org/10.2307/3054110.

3. Robert Longley, "What Is Procedural Justice?," ThoughtCo., April 27, 2022, https://www.thoughtco.com/what-is-procedural-justice-5225379.

4. Wilfred Lemke, "The Role of Sport in Achieving the Sustainable Development Goals," United Nations, accessed November 1, 2021, https://www.un.org/en /chronicle/article/role-sport-achieving-sustainable-development-goals.

5. Dana Reick, "Gardner Partners with Vera Institute to Reduce Racial Disparities in Legal System," *St. Louis American*, April 8, 2021, https://www.stlamerican.com /business/business_news/gardner-partners-with-vera-institute-to-reduce-racial -disparities-in-legal-system/article_b9e54fc4-98a8-11eb-b0a5-8bb4ab88394f.html.

6. Bel Rolley, "Behind the Jersey: We Must Address the Struggles of Black Women in Soccer," *Daily Trojan*, October 7, 2020, https://dailytrojan.com/2020/10/07 /behind-the-jersey-we-must-address-the-struggles-of-Black-women-in-soccer.

7. Steve Wartenberg, "In the News World of NIL, Luke Fedlam Guides Athletes on Money, Deals, and the Future, *Columbus CEO*, updated July 3, 2021, https://www.columbusceo.com/story/business/briefs/2021/07/01/college-athletes -and-nil-luke-fedlam-trusted-adviser/7577807002.

8. Kenneth J. Macri, "Not Just a Game: Sport and Society in the United States," *Inquiries* 4, no. 8 (2012): 1, http://www.inquiriesjournal.com/articles/1664/not-just-a -game-sport-and-society-in-the-united-states.

9. Jabari Young, "LA Clippers Sign $300-Million-Plus Arena Sponsorship Deal with Green Bank Aspiration," CNBC, September 27, 2021, https://www.cnbc

.com/2021/09/27/la-clippers-aspiration-sign-300-million-plus-arena-sponsor-deal.html.

10. Arshad Majeed, "LA Clippers, Aspiration Sign $300-Million-Plus Arena Sponsor Deal," *Verve Times*, September 27, 2021, https://vervetimes.com/la-clippers-aspiration-sign-300-million-plus-arena-sponsor-deal.

11. Kurt Streeter, "In Inglewood, Optimism and Anxiety Neighbor Super Bowl Stadium," *New York Times*, updated February 13, 2022, https://www.nytimes.com/2022/02/10/sports/football/where-is-the-super-bowl-2022.html.

12. Alicia Victoria Lozano and David K. Li, "Super Bowl Host Inglewood, California, Is Transforming on Multiple Fronts," NBC News, updated February 13, 2022, https://www.nbcnews.com/business/inglewood-demographic-changes-facts-diversity-rcna8227.

13. "NBA Legend and Prostate Cancer Survivor Kareem Abdul-Jabbar Featured in New Public Service Announcement by the Prostate Cancer Foundation and NBA Cares Launched on Father's Day," Prostate Cancer Foundation, June 21, 2021, https://www.pcf.org/news/nba-legend-and-prostate-cancer-survivor-kareem-abdul-jabbar-featured-in-new-public-service-announcement-by-the-prostate-cancer-foundation-and-nba-cares.

14. Yvonne Liu, "Disconnected Youth in Los Angeles," Advancement Project CA, March 28, 2018, https://www.advancementprojectca.org/blog/disconnected-youth-in-los-angeles.

15. "Tottenham Regeneration Is London's Biggest Growth Opportunity," *South China Morning Post*, May 28, 2018, https://www.scmp.com/presented/business/topics/invest-overseas-properties/article/2148046/tottenham-regeneration-londons.

16. Carlos Burgos, Victoria Alvarez, and Myfanwy Taylor, "We're Fighting to Show What Urban Development for People, Not Profit, Can Look Like," *Guardian*, August 11, 2021, https://www.theguardian.com/commentisfree/2021/aug/11/urban-development-for-people-not-for-profit-north-london-latin-village.

17. Meaghan Carey, Daniel S. Mason, and Laura Misener, "Social Responsibility and the Competitive Bid Process for Major Sporting Events," *Journal of Sport and Social Issues* 35, no. 3 (2011): 246–63, https://doi.org/10.1177/0193723511416985.

18. Matthew Stevens, "NFL Inks a 10-Year Stadium Partnership with Tottenham Hotspurs," *Baltimore Beatdown*, July 8, 2015, https://www.baltimorebeatdown.com/2015/7/8/8913305/nfl-inks-a-10-year-stadium-partnership-with-tottenham-hotspurs.

19. Sylvia Trendafiova, Vassilios Ziakas, and Emily Sparvero, "Linking Corporate Social Responsibility in Sport with Community Development: An Added Source of Community Value," *Sport in Society* 20, no. 7 (2017): 938–56, https://doi.org/10.1080/17430437.2016.1221935.

20. Jacob Ajom, "IWD 2021: NBA, BAL Launch Gender Equality Initiative in Africa," *Vanguard*, March 12, 2021, https://www.vanguardngr.com/2021/03/iwd-2021-nba-bal-launch-gender-equality-initiative-in-africa.

21. Shaun M. Anderson, "Creating a Collaborative Community Development Initiative," *Western City*, September, 4, 2018, https://www.westerncity.com/article/creating-collaborative-community-development-initiative.

22. IE Staff, "Colin Kaepernick's New Initiative Will Offer Free Autopsies for Those Killed in Police-Related Incidents," *Inside Edition*, February 24, 2022, https://www.insideedition.com/colin-kaepernicks-new-initiative-will-offer-free-autopsies-for-those-killed-in-police-related-73447.

23. Nashville SC Communications, "MLS Announces Updates and Enhancements to Diversity Hiring Policy," *Nashville SC*, December 7, 2021, https://www.nashvillesc.com/news/mls-announces-updates-and-enhancements-to-diversity-hiring-policy.

24. Rachel Treisman, "The U.S. National Women's Soccer Team Wins $24 Million in Equal Pay Settlement," NPR, February 22, 2022, https://www.npr.org/2022/02/22/1082272202/women-soccer-contracts-equal-pay-settlement-uswnt.

Index

About the Author

Shaun M. Anderson, PhD, is an associate professor of organizational communication at Loyola Marymount University. His work has been published in several academic journals and popular press outlets regarding sport, politics, and society. For more information, please visit www.shaunmarqanderson.com.